Jensen's Format Writing

How to Write Easily and Well

by

Frode Jensen

Dedicated to all my former teachers
who labored through my early efforts at writing.

4th printing 2006

ISBN 1-886061-29-7

FORMAT WRITING

Table of Contents

TO THE STUDENT

This book is concerned with developing expository writing skills. Other types of writing such as poetry, narrative or story telling, and certain types of business writing are not covered in this book. The skills taught here may have some carryover into other types of writing, but expository writing is the particular focus.

Expository writing is writing that exposes, puts forth, explains, reveals, or exhibits in detail about something. It has a purpose to inform, clarify, and perhaps even to persuade. Such writing may simply describe, or it may give a series of reasons. In any case there is a fundamental point that is made. How that point is made may often determine whether the piece is accepted or rejected. The purpose of this book is to give experience in various formats or organizational patterns so that whatever the point of a piece of writing, it will come across in a logical fashion and make the point as strongly as possible.

Writing can generally be broken down into four basic components: content, style, organization, and mechanics. Let's briefly review each of them.

Content is what is said, the subject of the writing and the various information given in the writing. Content is the sum and substance of the writing, the set of facts and the conclusion. It varies from paper to paper. Each new assignment generally means new content. Content is important. It is very difficult to write a good paper with poor content. The old saying, "You can't make a silk purse out of a sow's ear," applies quite well. The lesson to be learned here is that the subject of good writing must be one of recognizable worth, not something foolish or degrading. Content, as such, is not taught; however, your teacher will grade on it in some fashion. This book will give you some ideas about gathering information in useable form.

Style is the manner or expression of language. It is how something is said, the turns of phrase used by each writer. Style is something that is personal; it grows out of the writer and the writer's experience. Style is somewhat fluid or organic in that it changes as the writer matures. Some aspects of style can be taught; conciseness of expression and logical progression of thought are given some attention in this book. Because style is personal, different styles appeal to different readers and teachers. The grading of style is subjective and will vary somewhat according to each teacher.

Organization is how the material is put together; this book identifies a variety of formats or ways of organizing material. It is very teachable, but unfortunately it is generally not found in most books on writing. Every writing assignment carries with it two fundamental tasks: figuring out what to say and then organizing how it will be said. Mastering the procedures in this book will cut the work of future writing tasks in half. The first task is really getting the content together; the second task is primarily an organizational task although style and mechanics also have their part. This book deals with how to organize material into a cogent presentation. If the reader is able to follow an argument, then the reader is more likely to make a valid judgment on the content. Poorly organized thoughts convey negatives to the reader; this generally causes the reader to reject the argumentation of the writer. Incoherency in presentation not only distracts the reader, it detracts from the point the writer is attempting to make. The formats presented in this book provide ready-made templates into which content can be placed.

Mechanics comprise the technical aspects of writing: spelling, punctuation, and usage. Although not taught in this book, these areas are graded. Writing that is full of mechanical mistakes distracts the reader; any distractions to the reader weaken the paper. For help in punctuation see *Jensen's Punctuation*, another book by this author. Even neatness counts; a messy paper with erasures or a crumpled title page with stains on it makes a poor impression. Remember, what is written must stand by itself since the author is not there to help it along. With apologies to Hallmark Cards, "Care enough to write and turn in the very best."

This brief section is to encourage you. This book is a lot of work for you and your teacher, but it will pay off if you continue to give it good effort. Anyone can become a more effective writer; it simply takes some work. Do not be discouraged if the first few papers are marked up somewhat. Certain errors can be corrected with minor instruction. As mentioned above, each time you write you have two jobs to do: gathering the information and organizing it in the written form. You will learn how to do both in this class. The nice thing is that once you have mastered the organizational patterns, your work on all future writing assignments has literally been cut in half. The various formats are found throughout the book. That's why the book is called *Jensen's Format Writing*. Learn those formats now and use them for a lifetime.

Learn from your mistakes. Look carefully at your returned papers, and ask questions if you do not understand why something was marked. Becoming a good writer is a process, not single event. Good instruction, practice, and mastery of form all contribute to good writing. Good writing is clear writing that is generally free of mechanical difficulties; it should also be interesting, to the point, and have something of value to say.

Pay attention to the examples. They are given for your benefit. The examples are meant to teach you and further explain by example what the text has already told you. Read and study the examples before you do an assignment. As mentioned above, once you master the format, your only job is really just to dump your information into the format. The organization is mostly taken care of by the format itself.

Save some of your early papers and look at them after a number of weeks. You will be amazed at your improvement. Many of my students literally gasped when I told them they would be producing 1500 word papers with documentation every ten calendar days. Some later confided that they thought they could never do it. They all did and were thankful for the experience. Hang in there and learn. If you are curious, and you should be, read the section for the teacher that follows. It will help you understand how you will be graded.

TO THE TEACHER

The purpose of this section is to give you some ideas regarding this book. How you use the book will ultimately be up to you; the ideas given here are simply some ways, methods, and time frames that you might utilize.

The book falls naturally into seven basic sections. To do all of them in one year is possible, but both you and your students will be hard at work. The seven sections naturally align themselves into groups. The first section on single paragraphs can easily stand by itself. The next two sections both deal with the five paragraph essay and should be taught consecutively. The book reports and essay answers put the five paragraph formats to use. The business writing section is somewhat independent of the others. It uses formats, but they are of a different sort. You can use it at any point after the single paragraph section. The last two sections of the book also have a natural affinity in that the condensation principles are helpful practice for doing the research that often occurs when writing a paper of any length. In the past I have dealt with the material in two ways. When tutoring a group of home schoolers, I covered most of the material in a year and met with the students only one hour per week. It was difficult, but we managed. However, when I had a number of students in a series of classes, I covered the material over a period of two years, the break being after the practical application or business writing section depending on the time available and my stamina. Reading papers constantly is a challenge.

It is my contention that for the single paragraphs, the student should write at least three and perhaps five of each type of paragraph in order to instill the format. If the student is in class every day, a paragraph three times a week is good. That allows the teacher time to correct the writing and gives the student immediate feedback so improvements can be made while the student is in the process of learning the format. The Monday, Wednesday, Friday routine has worked well in the past for this section. Such a plan allows for other activities in the class but keeps the students writing on a regular basis. As a for instance, a new format can be explained on a Monday with the first paragraph to be handed in at the end of the period that day. Alternative deadlines might be the end of the school day or the beginning of the period on Tuesday or maybe even the next Wednesday if you take two weeks per format. You need some time to read the students' papers before they write their next paragraph. On Wednesday the first activity regarding writing should be to make some general comments about their writing; a mix of positives and negatives is generally the case. In a class situation, one or two papers might be read to highlight the remarks. The papers with the check sheets are then turned back; some individual conferencing is often appropriate. The next paragraph of that type is assigned, perhaps along with a specific topic, and an appropriate deadline is established. In the tutorial situation described previously, the students brought three paragraphs to the next meeting. The obvious disadvantage was they did not have any guidance except for the initial teaching; all remediation was after the fact. It was not the best situation.

The sections dealing with elements of five paragraph essays through the principle of condensation can simply be treated as individual assignments with one due per scheduled writing day. The non-writing days can be given over to literature or other activities. Literature generates many topics to write about, particularly ones assigned by the teacher.

In the five-paragraph essay section, I generally had the students write one essay per week. Personally, I introduced the new format on Wednesday and had the essays due the following Monday. That gave me a couple of days to read them and have them ready for comment and return the next Wednesday. If the students are going through the whole book in one year, it will be difficult for them to write more than one five paragraph essay of each type. My personal thought is that each type of essay should be practiced at least twice, and three times would be better. Individual circumstances will dictate the number and frequency of essays assigned. When introducing a new format, it is good to walk through the process with the students and answer any questions. The procedure as given in the book is quite easy to follow, but my students seemed to benefit from some oral interchange. As before, some individual conferencing with a student using the check sheet as a guide is often profitable. If I were teaching a single student or a very small number, I would conference with each one about every paper, even if I only spent a minute or two with some of them. Of course, while you are with one student, the others should be working.

The major paper section is the last teaching portion of the book. I use the terms *major paper*, *research paper*, and *position paper* somewhat interchangeably. This section is really quite open-ended. The first four papers are a building process in that a new element is added each time. There is no need to quit after the fourth paper if time permits others to be written. My philosophy is that the student will learn with practice, not with one big assignment. Permit me a personal observation at this point. The pattern in all the schools in which I was employed was to have the students write a research paper. It was a six to nine week ordeal with the grade being largely based on the final product. Secondary deadlines for outlines, note cards, rough drafts and so forth were imposed so the student would not try to do the whole thing at the last minute. Endless hours of class were expended in the library with little apparent learning going on. In fact, the whole exercise seemed to me to be one of frustration. Finally, all the papers would come in, and then I was buried for a time while I attempted to get them graded. However, an opportunity for change arose. At that point I opted for a new approach, a series of short papers that allowed practice in the various elements of paper writing. This, by the way, is simply applying a Biblical principle of learning, spaced repetition. The benefits were great. The students had opportunity to learn from their mistakes; they could get it right the second or third time and be rewarded for doing so. They practiced the procedures many times instead of just going through them once, so researching and organizing material became a familiar process to all and was mastered by many. As the teacher, I had the opportunity to review and comment on their writing much more often, and I was not stuck with a huge reading and grading job all at once. The real payoff was improved skills on the part of the students. Many of them came back while in college and thanked me for the edge they had over many of their classmates in college when it came to producing a written piece.

What about time frames for these larger papers? Two weeks is the maximum I would allow between papers. At one point while teaching a senior writing class, I required a 1500 word paper, typed and in good order, every ten calendar days. The students did have to work at it, but they were able to produce them right along. The practice is important. The length of the paper is somewhat immaterial; longer papers simply mean a longer time between papers. 1200-1500 words is a good length. It is long enough to require a bit of research and short enough so that a clear argument can be presented and evaluated readily. Additionally, each paper that is completed requires using all the skills of preparing a paper. As the teacher, you should provide the students with an overview at the beginning of course. The overview should contain the topics of each paper, the deadlines for each paper, the specific inclusions for each paper, and some general guidelines such as double spaced type, one side only, and other such things as you may require. That way everyone knows just what to expect. See the sample schedule at the end of this book. Such a schedule helps deal with absences and other disruptions.

Now it is time to discuss the analytical keys, the check sheets found at the back of the book. These can be duplicated as you see fit. You can use them directly or modify them for your own purposes. I have found these sheets quite valuable in establishing a grade and as tools for discussing a paper with a student. If you have a class situation with multiple students, the check sheets provide you with a set of quick notes in an organized form regarding your evaluation of any given paper. A student is also able to see the strengths and weaknesses regarding his or her paper in an easy and readable format.

First let's look at the **paragraph parameter check sheet**. This one is short and can be duplicated on a single sheet and cut in half to provide two check sheets. It would be good to have a copy of the check sheet in front of you as I go through it. I have provided two examples but will discuss only the first.

Under ORGANIZATION there are three entries. As you read a paragraph, check the blank if you believe the student has met the requirement. With me it was a check or a minus. A check meant they did the job; a minus meant I was not satisfied. The first and last blanks only involve one sentence each. The middle blank covers the body of the paragraph; that may be as many as five or six sentences. What about partial credit? I never gave it; the parameter says subsidiary sentences--that means all of them to me--fit the format; for me, they all had to fit to get the check.

The second section is labeled MECHANICS. You will note that I have broken it out into three areas: spelling, punctuation, and usage. In these blanks I would put the actual number of mistakes of each type that I found. On the student's paper, I would generally circle a misspelled word or write SP in the margin. Punctuation marks left out or incorrectly placed usually were circled or checked in the margin. Usage errors I marked in the margin with a U or made some other appropriate notation such as REF for improper reference. Any simple notation is fine so long as you and the student know what you are talking about. Usage errors always merited some comment during the personal conference time. After the number of errors is entered into the blanks, add them up. That number determines the total mechanics portion of the grade as given in the NOTE for the mechanics section. For instance, a paragraph with two spelling errors, a usage error and a punctuation error makes a total of four mistakes in mechanics. That translates to a -1 when adding up the points for the grade.

The third section is STYLE. Some of this is subjective. This is where the teacher or the grader of the paper can make a difference in the final grade. As in the first section, a check means the student merits your satisfaction. Each check is ultimately worth one point on the final grade scale. The last item in this section is called *balance in presentation*. This means two things: the length of the body sentences should be similar, and the level of ideas presented should be of near equal value. Many students grasp this very readily, but some seem to struggle with it constantly. It could be argued that this item should go under ORGANIZATION since it involves logic of a sort. Move it if you like.

The last section is CONTENT. In single paragraphs, the first two items are almost a repeat of those found under ORGANIZATION. There are differences, however. You will see it as you go along. Again, a check is rewarded if the student satisfies you that they met the requirement. Sometimes a student will leave out a fact that should be included. Sometimes they misuse or confuse ideas, and at times they will include sentences that are irrelevant or are totally off the wall. The second and third blanks take care of these errors.

Finally it is time to give the grade. Simply add up the items in sections one, three, and four. Put that total with the mechanics total of +1, 0, or -1. The resulting number will yield a letter grade. Under this system it is difficult for a student to fail if they turn in the paper and make a decent effort. On the other hand, they must do nearly everything right in order to get the A. The general pattern for my students in the past was that they improved and became more careful as time went on. With each new paragraph type, there is some early tendency to error in having the subsidiary sentences fit the format; this is because the format is new.

The COMMENT section is where you can say nice things, make notes to yourself and the student, and perhaps give a rewrite of part of a sentence to illustrate a point. The back of the check sheet is blank, so you can easily turn it over if you need the space. I always tried to write something. Examples might be "great topic sentence, conference necessary, good job, 4th sentence doesn't fit," and so on.

Now it is time to look at the **5 paragraph essay check sheet**. The basic idea is the same as the paragraph parameter check sheet, but the setup is a bit different.

The ORGANIZATION section is the longest, and it counts for half of the final grade. Organization, however, is what this book is all about, and it is what we are trying to teach; therefore, it forms a significant portion of the grade. The checklist is easy to follow since it moves from beginning to end through the essay. Award a check if the item is done to your satisfaction. Each item is pretty much a yes/no situation. Do they have an opening statement that is appropriate, ties in with the subject, and gets your attention? Does the introductory paragraph follow the general to specific pattern of organization? Is the purpose clearly stated in the thesis? Is the outline of the paper given in the thesis statement? Does the topic sentence of the first body paragraph come at the beginning of the paragraph and introduce the first item as stated in the thesis? Is there a proper transition between the introduction and the first body paragraph? And so goes the rest of it. Count up the check marks and circle the appropriate numbers in the scale on the right hand side of the sheet under ORGANIZATION.

The MECHANICS section is somewhat reduced in size on this sheet. You could easily redesign it to break out the three or four basic types of errors. With the existing form, it is necessary to count up the errors on the student's paper and then circle the appropriate set of numbers on the scale. When I had lots of papers to read, I would only mark errors to the sixth error. After the sixth error, I did not mark further errors simply to save time. If you only have one or a very few students, marking all the errors in the paper may be a better policy.

The EXPRESSION/CONTENT/READABILITY section is the subjective section; some might call it the teacher fudge faction. It is value judgment pure and simple. It is entirely up to each teacher as to how he/she uses this section. For me it meant how the paper came across in general, whether it lived up to my expectation of what the student is capable of, how clearly and forceful the argument was expressed, and whether the reasons were complete and proper. A comment is in order here. At times, an essay that is technically perfect still falls short of the mark. Other times a paper may make some marvelous statements and be quite superior except for some spelling or punctuation mistakes. This section allows the teacher some maneuvering territory when deciding the final grade. Use it wisely.

The COMMENT section is self-explanatory. The final grade is the sum of the three sections on the right of the check sheet. Another form, the **organizational format: student assessment form**, utilizes groups of three students to evaluate other student papers. You will find it among the check sheets. It is also helpful in understanding the 5 paragraph essay check sheet. Both of these forms are reproducible for multiple use.

I've provided you with a check sheet for one book report style, one for the business letters, and one for the resume. The idea is the same no matter what the assignment. You are looking for particular things in the work produced by the students, and how well they do determines the grade. The check sheets I have provided are models; they are not set in stone. You can and perhaps should make up some of your own. Once you grasp the beauty of the check sheet or analytical key, you should become sold on it. You can tailor these for almost any assignment.

The major paper check sheets have three variations and are sequential. The third check sheet should be used for all papers after the second paper. The FORM area is expanded to include each new item as it is introduced. That is the only difference between the three check sheets. Annotated works cited are simply included under the works cited section. All items on this check sheet except the FORM section are replicated from the earlier check sheets, so I will not review them again. The FORM section is new, however. You will note that by each item there is a series of numbers: 0 1 2. My standard for assigning these numbers is as follows: 2 means the student has completed that item with no mistakes; 1 means the student has completed the item, but it needs some improvement; 0 means either it was not done or was done so poorly that no credit can be given. Obviously some value judgments will have to be made regarding these items. As time goes on, the student will have more time to practice; thus, the standards can be raised over time.

The tests that are included with this book are self-explanatory. Keys are provided as well as grading scales where appropriate. Directly after the 5 paragraph essay check sheet you will find a student assessment form regarding organizational structure. After the third or fourth five paragraph essay, you can begin to have your students critique the essays of others using this form. I put the students in groups of three or four and had them evaluate a set of papers. Each student in the group had to read every paper. I encouraged them to compare and discuss their evaluations after they finished. This form will help them to see the organizational patterns in writing; it really is a teaching tool. You will have to decide if the student evaluations will be a part of the grade on the essay or not. Also at the end of the book you will find a couple of sample schedules I used on two different occasions. Use them as guides for constructing something similar for your students.

This has been a rather long section to read, but it is very important that some method of consistent grading be adopted for student writing. The method employed should also point out the strengths and weaknesses in each student's writing. The check sheet method does both. The added benefit is that it is easy for the teacher to use once you understand it. If fact, a good check sheet system should reduce the time you have to spend grading papers unless you just give a student paper a cursory read and plop a grade on it. Surely you are more conscientious than that. May you use the check sheets along with this book to improve the writing of your student or students as the case may be. To God be the glory.

SECTION 1

Single Paragraph Formats

PARAGRAPHS

This section of the book will deal with paragraphs. The first two pages have some general information you should read and digest. Then there is a short section on continuity in writing. You will also find a page dealing with how the paragraphs will be evaluated. Following that you will find information on seven basic formats or organizational patterns expository paragraphs follow. Those formats are what you will practice and turn in. They represent the meat of this particular section.

Single paragraphs are usually written in school or as brief descriptions in catalogues. Most of the rest of the time paragraphs are linked with one another to form some sort of lengthier piece. In a school situation you are often asked to write a paragraph on this or that subject; sometimes you are asked to respond with a paragraph for an answer on a test. Being able to write a tight paragraph that expresses your ideas well is a good skill to have. After practicing the paragraph formats in this book, you should be able to produce a paragraph on demand with minimal effort and still have it come across well to the reader.

The seven basic formats you will find in this book are time-honored methods of organization; they are not something that this author made up. On the other hand, most students never have these organizational patterns identified by their teachers and are left to shift for themselves as to how to put their ideas together. Each of the patterns you will learn is unique and serves a particular purpose. However, most subjects can be organized in a variety of ways, so there is some overlap. Your job after you finish this book will be to decide which pattern to use when faced with writing about a given subject. You will know the basic formats, and one or two of them will always fit a given subject. You will find that some subjects lend themselves to one particular format while others can be organized in a variety of fashions.

Does everyone use patterns in their writing? Yes, almost everyone organizes their thoughts on paper to some degree; at times, however, the patterns may not be readily discernible. Does everyone consciously sit down and decide what format to follow? No, very few people spend much time in deciding a particular format to follow; they just write as the information and inspiration come. Such writing is generally somewhat loose in its structure. Those who consciously outline their ideas according to a given pattern are often rewarded with a more tightly organized piece of writing and one that is more effective in its impact.

For each of the formats that follow, your teacher will ask you to write a number of paragraphs that conform to the organizational pattern. The subject matter will vary. Each format is presented with a set of ideas, a series of steps to produce such a paragraph, an example, an assignment your teacher might modify, and some sample topics. Read the format pages carefully and follow the instructions given both in the book and any additional ones imposed by your teacher. Some practice in each format will familiarize you with each type and help you understand the process of organizing ideas according to that format as well as in general.

ESSENTIALS OF GOOD PARAGRAPHS

INTRODUCTION: Structure and development of the paragraph

Unless a piece of writing is extremely short, it is usually divided into parts called paragraphs consisting of several sentences and offset from the rest of the materials by indentation or spacing. A paragraph is not only a physical division; it also is a unit of the writer's thought used to show which sentences are closely related. Additionally, it is a series of sentences developing only one topic, a new paragraph being used for each new topic. The important parts of paragraph development are listed below. This information applies to paragraphs that stand alone without reference to any other writing and to body paragraphs of any multiple paragraph essay.

1. Topic Sentences

   A. usually at the beginning of the paragraph, introduces the topic
   B. tells the reader what the paragraph is about, states the purpose
   C. gives unity to the paragraph

2. Body

   A. a series of supporting sentences explaining the topic sentence
   B. contains details, examples, incidents, facts, and reasons which support the topic sentence
   C. generally developed by any of seven common methods
   D. has unity and coherence

      1) clear, logical sequence of events

         a) chronological order of time
         b) spatial order (by position)
         c) order of importance

      2) transitional devices

         a) chronological words: *first, second, meanwhile, later, afterward, finally,* etc.
         b) spatial words: *next to, in front of, beside, between, behind,* etc.
         c) other words expressing relationships of ideas: *however, nevertheless, in fact, yet, because,* etc.

      3) completeness

         a) free of mechanical and spelling errors
         b) correct grammar usage
         c) correct sentence structure

3. Conclusion or clincher

   A. end of the paragraph
   B. restates or sums up the topic sentence in different words

GOOD PARAGRAPH PRACTICES

The following information is to be applied particularly to paragraphs but has application to longer works as well. Once a point of view or tense is adopted, it should be retained throughout the exposition, be it a paragraph or a lengthier piece. Subordination of ideas also applies albeit in a more expanded manner. Sentences within a paragraph are akin to paragraphs within an essay; in other words, there is a hierarchy of ideas and their organization; these are replicated from the paragraph to the essay as a whole.

Point of view

Point of view is perspective, the person in which the writing is expressed. There are three persons: first, second, and third. First person is the person speaking. In this case the sentences use pronouns such as *I, me, my, our,* and *we.* Use of the first person when writing generally lends a highly personal tone to the work. Second person is the person being spoken to, *you* and its associated pronouns. Use of the second person in writing gives the work an exhortative tone; the writer is telling the audience directly. Third person is the person being spoken about; pronouns such as *he, her, him, it, they, their,* and *his* are used in this situation. Using the third person in writing lends a somewhat objective or impersonal tone to the writing. The rule is to be consistent. A writer can pick any of the three perspectives. In fact, different objectives and topics in the writing lend themselves to particular perspectives. Once a perspective is adopted, however, that perspective should not be shifted. The key here is to monitor the subjects of sentences and check to see that each and every subject follows suit. Not following suit is an error; it commonly falls under improper usage and is often marked as *person shift.*

Tense

Tense is a grammatical category; there are two tenses: past and present. The first verb in any verb combination or cluster shows the tense. The rule is to remain in the same tense during the entire paragraph or essay. Shifting around is cause for confusion and is regarded as an usage error. It is often marked as *tense shift.* Such an error is easy to make but also easy to correct with a careful proofreading. Just monitor the first verbs in the sentences and see if they agree in tense.

Subordination of ideas

The topic sentence in a paragraph typically makes a statement that needs support. That support comes in the rest of the paragraph via the other sentences. All sentences in the paragraph should be subordinate to the main idea expressed in the topic sentence. Two general organizational patterns are acceptable. The first is that all sentences are equally balanced sub-points. For instance, each sentence may contain a different example that supports the topic sentence. The second method is that each sentence that makes a sub-point also has a sentence which follows that further elaborates on that particular sub-point. In essence a second level of subordination in the paragraph exists. Both methods are given in outline form below. Note that each sentence on a given level should have a rough equality in importance to other sentences on that level.

Pattern #1	Pattern #2
Topic sentence	Topic sentence
sub-point 1	sub-point 1
sub-point 2	elaboration
sub-point 3	sub-point 2
sub-point 4	elaboration
conclusion	conclusion

CONTINUITY IN WRITING

One problem found in student writing, particularly that of younger students, is the lack of continuity. By that I mean the sentences do not flow well together; they don't tie well to one another.

The difficulty for the reader is to put it together in a reasonable fashion. This should not be the reader's job; it is the job of the writer to make an organized presentation. In fact, the better the organization, the more able the reader is absorb the content, which is generally the writer's purpose.

Many people often write as they think; this is especially true with younger children. The problem is that thoughts are often scattered instead of logically ordered. I remember my mother saying to me numerous times, "What has that got to do with the price of tea in China?" Of course, she was telling me in her elliptical fashion that my most recent statement had no relation to what I had previously said.

So, how do you know if you have a logical progression of thought in your writing? I maintain you can see it through the structure of the writing. Below you will find a series of ideas that are simple and can be easily followed by all students. I'm only making one assumption, that the students can recognize a noun when they see it. That's pretty basic, and almost all students can do so.

What follows will be obvious when I explain it. Unfortunately, many times the obvious is not taught; instead it is assumed. That's a common problem with teaching. Experience has shown me that explaining the obvious pays big dividends. Not all students know the things their teachers assume they know.

The key to having continuity in writing is repetition. Something from the previous sentence needs to be repeated in some fashion. Here are a few of the obvious ways of making reference from one sentence to another.

First all writing must begin somewhere. Thus, the first sentence will make some statement about something. A general idea or a main idea will be identified. Subsequent sentences will build on or explain this idea in some way. Therefore, those subsequent sentences need ties to previous sentences. Here's how it works.

1. The easiest method is to simply repeat the subject. Two successive sentences share the same subject.

> Joe went to town. Joe met Sally.

In the above, we have *Joe* as the subject. First he goes to town, a simple action. Then he meets Sally, another simple action, but we have moved the writing forward and kept our continuity.

2. The second method, and one which is really a variant on the first, is to repeat the subject but use a pronoun reference instead of repeating the actual noun. This lends variety and efficiency to the writing.

> Joe went to town. He met Sally.

3. A third variant would be to repeat the subject but use a synonym instead of the original noun. Not all subjects lend themselves to this method, but enough do so that it can be used rather often.

> Joe and his brothers went to town. The boys met Sally.

4. Thus far, we have kept our repetition to the subject, but things wouldn't get very far were we to stay on that tack. The fourth method, not a variant of the others, is to repeat one of the other nouns from the previous sentence.

> Joe went to town. Going to town was a major event.

Obviously in the above *town* is repeated. I am using very simple sentences. Think of all the possibilities in the following sentence.

> Joe met Sally on his way to town after the ball game on Saturday.

Look at all the nouns in the above sentence. Any one of them could be repeated. Of course, each noun would probably move the discourse in a new direction. Picking *Sally* instead of *ball game* as the new subject would certainly shift the emphasis.

5. This is a variant on the previous method. Instead of repeating the noun as a noun, use a pronoun.

> Joe went to town. It was the only place to get supplies.

6. The sixth method is to substitute a pronoun for a summary of some part of the previous sentence.

> Joe went to town. It was an all day affair.

Here we see that the second sentence is referring to the whole idea of Joe going to town.

You will note that all substitutions or references in the second sentence thus far are in the subject position. This is the logical place for the repeated or referenced item to appear since it becomes the focus of attention for the new sentence. Other possibilities exist.

7. The seventh method requires the repetition of some other part of the sentence, usually the predicate, often with a noun in it.

> Joe went to town. We also went to town.
> Joe ran around the house. We ran around the garage.

In the above we have the actions being repeated, either directly or in a slightly different manner.

> Joe ran over to the slide. We walked over to the swings.

Here we see the action being contrasted. It is still a repetition of structure; it mimics the action but does it with different words.

8. The eighth method is use transitional words such as *first, next, then*, and others like them. This method is usually found when explaining a process.

> First go outside. Then look up in the sky.

Of course, as some of you would rightly point out, the above example has the same subject for both sentences. It just isn't stated, but *you* is understood as the subject.

CONTINUITY EXERCISES

DIRECTIONS: Write a second sentence following the directions given. Your sentences must tie in to the sentence given previous to the instruction.

John brought home a rose for his mother.

1. repeat the subject

2. repeat the subject as a pronoun

3. repeat *home* as the new subject

4. repeat *rose* as the new subject

5. repeat *mother* as the new subject

6. use mother as the new subject but as a pronoun

My dog likes to chase rabbits in the field by our house.

7. use a synonym of *dog* for the subject

8. repeat *rabbits* as the new subject

9. repeat *field* as the new subject

10. repeat *house* as the new subject

Alfred drove the bus to the local church.

11. repeat the subject

12. repeat the subject as a pronoun

13. use a transitional word and use *children* as the new subject

14. use *bus* as the new subject

15. use *church* as the new subject

16. repeat a part of the predicate with a new subject

17. use a repetition of action in some way

18. use a summary of part of the sentence

Who
What
When
Where
Why
How

sequence of events — then what? what?

PARAGRAPH PARAMETER CHECKS

An analytical key such as those in the back of the book or something like them will be developed by your teacher and used as a check sheet for your paragraphs. I suggest writing about something you are currently studying in Bible, science, history, or literature. Of course, your teacher may pick your topics for you. If not, you can pick your own topics, but it is good to write about what you are learning in other subjects since it helps you to both digest and retain the information. In effect, it helps your study in your other courses. It goes without saying that the subjects you do write upon should be in good taste and should reflect your best efforts. Last minute efforts and improper or inane subject material are examples of shoddy craftsmanship and are not acceptable. Do your best.

Be careful of mechanics. If there are too many problems in that area, it detracts greatly from your writing and leaves a bad impression on the reader. According to the check sheets in the back, poor mechanics can cost you up to a full grade.

After you have written your paragraph, it is best to let it rest a day or two if you have the time; then proofread it for mistakes. You should even read it out loud; that helps to catch certain errors. Be sure to read what you have actually written, not just what you want it to say. The advantage of the time delay between writing and proof reading is that you will be more inclined to read it as it is instead of reading into it what you want since it is not as fresh in your mind as when you had just written it. If possible, it is to your advantage to have someone else read your paragraph and make comment. He/she is limited to what you have written and will read the piece for what it actually says. You should reciprocate by reading the other person's work if he/she is a fellow student.

Please note that the check sheets have four basic areas: organization, mechanics, style, and content. Each one of these areas contributes to or detracts from your overall grade. The purpose of the check sheet is to give you and your teacher specific information regarding your strengths and weaknesses. This allows you to concentrate on improving the areas that need work. In fact, you might construct a grid upon which you can place the numbers or marks from each check sheet. Over time this will allow you and your teacher to see a pattern in your errors. That will then further help your concentration on those areas of identified weaknesses.

Pay particular attention to whatever specifics are given on any particular assignment. Those specifics often make or break a paragraph. Good writing requires some attention to detail. You have been forewarned.

Pay attention to what the teacher has marked on the check sheets and any remarks in the comment section. Your performance in the various areas determines your final grade. Most of the areas are fairly cut and dried; that is, you either did or did not perform the task. A few do call for some judgment on the part of the teacher. As a student, you will have to determine what the teacher's preferences are and adjust accordingly. Each teacher is somewhat different. Those sections, however, should not count for more than a single step in the final grade.

You will find parameter check sheets for all of your writing. They will change to include other items as the writing assignments become longer and more complicated. The check sheets will also provide you and your teacher a common ground for discussing your writing.

Now just an advance note of warning. The first two formats seem to be alike, but they are not. The example format asks for examples. If the topic were pickup trucks, the examples might be Ford, Toyota, Datsun, and Dodge. The classification model says to put the pickup in a series of categories: manufacturers, typical users, the various sizes of pickups, and perhaps the uses of a pickup. This model is not a rehash of examples.

THE EXAMPLE PARAGRAPH

The example paragraph is used to provide a better understanding of a subject by seeing various examples of it. The subjects can vary from physical objects to concepts. Horses, chairs, honesty, and dictatorships could all be topics of an example paragraph.

BASIC REQUIREMENTS:

1) All examples should be relevant to the subject.
2) The examples should be familiar to most people.

OTHER ITEMS OF IMPORTANCE:

1) Be sure the examples are clear and appropriate to your point.
2) Look for a natural order if any among your examples.
3) For each example, provide some extra information in the sentence.
4) Avoid complicated subjects for a single paragraph; such topics are better suited for
   multi-paragraph essays.

METHOD OF CONSTRUCTION:

1) pick a topic
2) brainstorm for examples
3) pick best examples; eliminate repetitions & unsuitable ideas
4) arrange the order of the examples
5) generate a topic sentence
6) utilize the examples in the body of the paragraph
7) write a concluding sentence

WORKING IT THROUGH:

1) The topic will be root crops.
2) Here are some examples of root crops: beets, carrots, radishes, parsnips, onions, turnips, sugar beets, potatoes, and peanuts.
3) Let's pick beets, carrots, radishes, turnips and potatoes; they are well known and all have some different characteristics. The number of examples we need to pick is dependent on the number of sentences required in the body paragraph. Remember, we always need an introduction and conclusion as well. There are two ways we could do this paragraph. First, we could have a different example for each body sentence. Second, we could have two sentences for each example if we had enough to say about each example. We'll use the first type this time.
4) We need to arrange the order for these items. Perhaps it could be by size of the root; maybe it could be by popularity. Perhaps it could be length of time from planting to harvest. We should always have some logical order to our examples. For this example, let's use size of the root, and let's arrange it from smallest to largest. The probable order would radish, carrot, beet, turnip, and potato. We are talking average size here.
5) Now we need to generate a topic sentence, something about roots in general and hopefully something that reflects our order of arrangement. Root crops, which are found in most home gardens, vary in size and use.
6) We need to write a sentence about each root in the order we have placed them. See the example.
7) The concluding sentence should make some summary or motivational statement about our subject.

EXAMPLE #1:

Root Crops for the Household Garden

Root crops, which are found in most home gardens, vary in size and use. Many people grow radishes since they are rather small and grow very quickly. Carrots are a long root and require loose soil to do well. Beets vary in size from golf ball size to baseball size and are best before they get woody. Turnips are about the same size as beets, but now they are not nearly as popular as they once were. Perhaps the best know root crop is the potato; it takes lots of room to grow, but it yields a nice harvest most people enjoy. From the marble sized radish to the large baking potato, root crops are an important part of our diets which can easily be grown at home in a household garden.

EXAMPLE #2:

Here's another paragraph about root crops, but it is organized according to the second method mentioned previously on page 14. It will have two sentences about each example instead of one. We'll just use radishes, beets, and potatoes to get our six internal sentences.

Root Crops for the Household Garden

Root crops, which are found in most home gardens, vary in size and use. Radishes are generally the smallest of the root crops except for some of the large Japanese radishes. Most home gardeners use the small red radishes since they are quick and easy to grow and take very little space. Beets are also red in color, but they are larger than radishes, more like golf ball to baseball size. Home gardeners like beets since they provide both a root and a leaf crop. Potatoes can get quite large, many being bigger than softballs, but they do take up lots of space in the garden. If the household garden has plenty of space, home grown potatoes can produce a big harvest that can be used over a period of time. Root crops, which can easily be grown at home in a household garden, are an important part of our diets, and they are often tastier that what you can buy in the store.

ASSIGNMENT #1:

Write an example paragraph composed of seven sentences. The first sentence will be the topic sentence; the five body sentences will provide five different examples, and the last sentence will provide a conclusion of some sort.

SAMPLE TOPICS: types of horses, computer games, board games, card games, household pets, favorite dinners, historical novels, baseball players or teams, Bible characters, game birds, football plays, all terrain vehicles, types of cars, hymns or songs, flower types, trees, and so forth. These are just samples. You can make up your own topics, or your teacher can assign different ones. Be creative.

ASSIGNMENT #2:

Write an example paragraph composed of eight sentences. The first sentence will be the topic sentence; use two sentences for each example in the body paragraph as was done in Example #2; the last sentence should be a concluding sentence.

SAMPLE TOPICS: see the samples and the note above.

THE CLASSIFICATION PARAGRAPH

Classification is the orderly arrangement of items or ideas. Its purpose is to categorize an item, to place it along with others in its class so that the reader can do likewise. Being able to put an item with a group allows the reader to assign a whole set of parameters to it while putting it in place.

The classification format is different from the example format. The example format requires the student to produce a series of examples about a given topic. The classification format does not request examples; it needs details that place the topic into a particular class. An outline of each type using the same topic will be helpful to illustrate.

Our topic for illustration will be pickup trucks. In the example format, the examples could easily be producers of pickups such as Toyota, Chevy, Dodge, Nissan, and so forth. A sentence about each type of pickup would amply fulfill the example model.

The classification model is somewhat different. One sentence could give examples of a few manufacturers such as those given above in the example format. Another sentence might mention the primary use of pickup trucks, light hauling. A third sentence could state who drives such pickups: farmers, contractors, hunters, and fishermen. A fourth sentence might mention the various sizes such trucks come in. The fifth sentence could handle other variations such as 4x4, dual wheels, flatbed conversions, and so forth.

The classification model provides a method that allows the writer to describe the topic by placing it in a variety of categories. It is not just a variety of the example model.

BASIC REQUIREMENTS:

    1) The categories or subdivisions should be of equal value.
    2) The categories should be familiar, clear and helpful.

OTHER ITEMS OF IMPORTANCE:

    1) The subjects will usually be kinds or types of people, places or things, what is normally called nouns.
    2) All categories should follow some logical and natural order, time space, size, value, composition, *etc.*
    3) Similarities should be stressed since like items are placed together.
    4) Stereotyping is an example of overuse of classification.
    5) Avoid complicated subjects for a single paragraph; such topics are better suited for
         multi-paragraph essays.

METHOD OF CONSTRUCTION:

    1) pick a topic to classify
    2) decide the common element on which the categorization depends
    3) brainstorm for categories
    4) decide the major categories or subdivisions you will use
    5) arrange them in order of probable use
    6) generate a topic sentence
    7) provide the details by category for the body of the paragraph
    8) write a concluding sentence

WORKING IT THROUGH:

1) Bows will be the topic.

2) The common element will be what is available today in America, modern bows.

3) Here are some ideas: style, makers, materials, accessories, use, popularity, weights available.

4) For our purposes here, let's use style, makers, materials, use, and accessories. Each of these categories has a number of examples we can use or something we can expand upon, so that is good.

5) When putting the five categories in order, we should look for some kind of flow from one category to another. Let's do it this way: materials, style, use, makers, and accessories.

6) We need a topic sentence; it should say something about today to indicate our focus on modern bows. The bow and arrow combination is an ancient weapon that is still in use today.

7) We need to provide details for each topic.

    materials: fiberglass, metal, laminates including wood and other combinations

    style: compound, reflex, re-curve

    use: hunting, fishing, target practice – recreational in America

    makers: Shakespeare, Browning, Bear, Pearson, many others

    accessories: quivers, sights, releases, fishing reels, etc.

EXAMPLE:

Bows of Today

The bow and arrow combination is an ancient weapon that is still in use today. Modern materials have replaced the wood and horn of old, so today bows are made of fiberglass, metal, and various laminates including some woods. Bows now come in various styles such as the re-curve, reflex, and compound bows, but the compound bow is most popular today. The traditional uses of the bow are still in vogue, namely hunting, target shooting, and some fishing; it is no longer used as a weapon of war in America. Some modern bow manufacturers are Shakespeare, Bear, Pearson, and Browning, but other popular brands also exist. Multiple accessories also are available; they include quivers, sights, releases, fishing reels, and a variety of other items. The great array of choices available for the modern bow hunter shows that bows are still very popular today.

ASSIGNMENT:

Write a classification paragraph composed of seven sentences. The first sentence will be the topic sentence; the five body sentences will identify the subdivisions, and the last sentence will provide a conclusion of some sort.

SAMPLE TOPICS: fishing lures, romance stories, cartoon characters, cakes, Old Testament kings, computers, a kind of church music such as traditional hymns or maybe choruses, a type of dancing like clogging or the waltz, a Native American group from the Southwest or wherever, great vacation spots in some geographical area. Be creative again but remember that you are looking for a kind of type of something. Don't write another example paragraph.

THE DEFINITION PARAGRAPH

The definition is used to clarify understanding. Its purpose is to present a clear meaning of an abstract term so that the reader will know what you mean when you use the term.

BASIC REQUIREMENTS:

1) The definition should utilize at least three ways to define terms.
2) The categories should be clear and understandable.

OTHER ITEMS OF IMPORTANCE:

1) Try to utilize terms in the definition that are commonly understood rather than terms which also need defining by most people.
2) A logical progression in the definition should be observed; make it flow from one point to the next.
3) Any word used as a word out of context must always be underlined or italicized.
4) Avoid complicated subjects for a single paragraph; such topics are better suited for multi-paragraph essays.

METHOD OF CONSTRUCTION:

1) pick a term/idea to define
2) list all synonyms and antonyms that come to mind
3) identify closely related terms & their differences
4) give an example or two of the term
5) identify any meanings associated with the term
6) arrange the order of the points you will use
7) generate a topic sentence
8) use the various definitions in the body of the paragraph
7) write a concluding sentence

WORKING IT THROUGH:

1) The topic will be faith.
2) Various synonyms would be *belief, trust, confidence*, and *reliance*. Other meanings would be *religion* or *creed*. Note that words used out of context, that is words used as words, are italicized or underlined. They are not put in quotes. Antonyms would be *faithless, unbelief, doubt*, and *mistrust*. A Thesaurus is helpful for this portion.
3) Closely related terms: *hope, philosophy of life*. These imply less conviction, less definitiveness.
4) Martyrs are commonly known for their faith. People who have a great zeal for some cause are examples of those having lots of faith. In some instances people have a strong faith in something they can't prove.
5) Associated meanings would have to do with fervency of belief, often in some sort of religion or deeply held convictions.
6) Arrange the order of the points we will use; let's try for some flow: antonyms first, then synonyms and closely related terms, then associated meanings and finally examples.
7) Generate a topic sentence. *Faith* is a term often used by religious people, so we will explore its meanings.
8) Use the various definitions in the body of the paragraph. See the example below.
9) Write a concluding sentence that is either a summary or a motivational statement. This should not be done until the paragraph is finished since we need to know what is said in order to finalize it.

EXAMPLE:

The Meaning of Faith

Faith is a term often used by religious people, so we will explore its meanings. Faith is the opposite of unbelief, mistrust, and doubt; faith is not a strong skepticism and an unwillingness to be brought around to a position. Faith is synonymous with terms such as *belief* and *trust*; and at times it also means a particular religion or creed. Faith is similar to having a philosophy of life, but having faith indicates basic truths that seem deeper than a mere philosophy. Faith and hope are similar, but faith is stronger, more intense, perhaps even more tenacious. The idea of faith is often associated with some fervency in belief, a willingness to go against the crowd for a strongly held idea or ideal. In history we see many examples of people who died willingly because of their faith in God; they were committed to act upon that faith no matter what the consequences might be. Every Christian by definition should have a strong faith in Christ.

ASSIGNMENT:

Write a definition paragraph composed of seven or eight sentences. The first sentence will be the topic sentence; the internal body sentences define your term, and the last sentence will provide a conclusion of some sort.

SAMPLE TOPICS: freedom, love, fear, happiness, success, poverty, honesty, greed, friendship, education, business, work, etc. Note that you are picking some topic that you can define by various means to make it clear what you mean when you use the term.

Note that you will have lexical definitions, those that come from the dictionary; these will be both synonyms and antonyms since you can define something by what it is not as well as by what it is. You will have some associated meanings, ideas that flow from and are closely related to the term you choose. With these you need to differentiate, explain the slight differences and the associations between your term and these closely related terms and ideas. Finally you should have some examples people can relate to. You may use one or two sentences for each of these three categories of definitions as you see fit.

THE PROCESS PARAGRAPH

There are two basic variations:
 a) giving simple directions by telling someone how to do something, and
 b) giving information about how some process was or is to be accomplished.

BASIC REQUIREMENTS:

1) All steps must be in the correct order. (time order)
2) All vital steps must be included.

OTHER ITEMS OF IMPORTANCE:

1) Be careful about assuming too much regarding the reader's prior knowledge of the subject.
2) Attempt to make the instructions both clear and interesting.
3) Avoid lengthy or complicated procedures as subjects for a single paragraph; such topics are better suited for multi-paragraph essays.

METHOD OF CONSTRUCTION:

1) pick a topic
2) brainstorm
3) group and arrange the steps chronologically
4) decide whether you are giving directions or information
5) generate a topic sentence
6) describe the process in the body of the paragraph
7) write a concluding sentence

WORKING IT THROUGH

1) Let's talk about hunting, driving pheasants with a group of hunters.
2) Now we need to brainstorm for ideas: what kind of field, where to start the hunt, how to place the hunters to start, where the hunters will end up, how they will move, how to judge the field, safety factors.
3) Put the items in order of sequence: a) figure out what field to hunt, what type of field, b) decide on the starting point and formation of the hunters, c) explain and execute the plan, d) make sure of the safety precautions regarding placement of the hunters.
4) Since this is a general situation, I will give information that could be adapted to a variety of situations.
5) Generate a topic sentence: One effective way to hunt pheasants is to set up a drive through a field planted in corn, cotton, or some tall grains.
6) Describe the process in the body of the paragraph: write out sentences that flow in the order of the process: select shooting end & place hunters; form the rest of the hunters at the other end; move through the field; the stationed hunters should move to keep the birds from running out; get set to shoot when everyone is close.
7) Write a concluding sentence: Hunting a field in this manner usually provides plenty of action with birds flying in all directions.

EXAMPLE:

Driving Pheasants in a Planted Field

One effective way to hunt pheasants is to set up a drive through a field planted in corn, cotton, or some tall grains. One end of the field is selected as the shooting end, and one or two hunters are placed there just outside the field. The rest of the hunters form a diagonal line and enter the field at the opposite end. They move slowly forward so as to push the birds in front of them. The hunters on the shooting end should move back and forth across the end to stop the pheasants from running out of the field. When everyone gets close together at the end, some birds will flush, and the shooting will begin in earnest. Hunting a field in this manner usually provides plenty of action with birds flying in all directions.

ASSIGNMENT:

Write a process paragraph composed of seven sentences. The first sentence will be the topic sentence; the five body sentences will briefly outline the process, and the last sentence will provide a conclusion of some sort.

SAMPLE TOPICS: cleaning a fish, giving a speech, how to apply for a job, how to plant a tree or shrub, giving a perm to someone, baking cookies, planning a family vacation, how to win at Monopoly, a simple bicycle repair, an efficient way to mow the lawn, how to witness to a friend, how to study for a test, five steps to a successful coin collection, how to do a character study, how to run a meeting, the way to present a top water bass lure. Any topic that will break down into a series of steps is a likely candidate for this type of paragraph. Remember, it is only a paragraph, so keep it simple.

THE ANALOGY PARAGRAPH

The analogy is used to describe one subject in terms of another. Its purpose is to illustrate the strange or unknown in terms of the familiar. An example of an analogy would be describing the heart in terms of a pump. There is usually only a partial similarity, but it is enough to clarify the point. Often the two items will have a similarity of process or function.

BASIC REQUIREMENTS:

    1) All comparisons should be in terms of one another.
    2) One of the subjects should be familiar to most people.

OTHER ITEMS OF IMPORTANCE:

    1) Be sure the two subjects are comparable, have meaningful things in common.
    2) Decide if the analogy will help clarify the subject being described.
    3) Avoid complicated subjects for a single paragraph; such topics are better suited for multi-paragraph essays.

METHOD OF CONSTRUCTION:

    1) pick a topic to describe
    2) find an object for comparison that is well known
    3) brainstorm for similarities
    4) arrange the order of the points you will use
    5) generate a topic sentence
    6) describe the subjects in the body of the paragraph
    7) write a concluding sentence

WORKING IT THROUGH

1) The topic will be the heart and the blood system.
2) The heart is really a natural pump, so let's make an analogy with a mechanical pump.
3) **Brainstorming** we find the following: both the heart & the pump move a fluid; the fluid flows in a closed system; the fluid flows by pressure, the fluid flows through pipes, valves control the fluid movement.
4) **Arrange an order:** first we can make a general statement or two, and then we can describe the fluid movement and what takes place; fluids are moved by pressure with a system of valves; the heart/pump is central in a closed system.
5) **Generate a topic sentence:** The heart is an indispensable organ in the human body because it moves the blood around the body.
6) **Describe the subjects in the body paragraph:** put a series of sentences together based on #4.
7) **Write a concluding sentence:** The human blood system is a closed system with continuous pressure because our heart is always pumping to keep the blood flowing.

EXAMPLE:

Understanding the Working of the Heart

The heart is an indispensable organ in the human body because it moves the blood around the body. The heart in effect is the central pumping station of the body and acts as the major pump that pushes and pulls the blood through the arteries and veins. The common pump operates with a valve to let liquid into a chamber; so does the heart. Once the pump chamber is full, the valve or flap closes. Then the pump puts pressure on the liquid to force it out of the chamber through another valve, and this happens to us when our heart contracts. The liquid, or in our case, the blood, is then forced out to circulate through the system. The human blood system is a closed system with continuous pressure because our heart is always pumping to keep the blood flowing.

ASSIGNMENT:

Write an analogy paragraph composed of seven sentences. The first sentence will be the topic sentence; the five body sentences will make the comparisons, and the last sentence will provide a conclusion of some sort.

SAMPLE TOPICS: eye & lens, mouth & speaker, valve & door, city government & ant hill, high rise office & bee hive, brain & computer, life and a play as in Shakespeare's monologue on the seven ages of man, life as a journey, life as a river flowing through time, the Holy Spirit and the wind, preparing a meal and preparing a speech, building a house and preparing a report, laying out a garden or a city plan.

THE CAUSE & EFFECT PARAGRAPH

The cause and effect paragraph is used to explain why something occurred. It gives reasons why some event has happened or perhaps why it will happen in the future. This type of paragraph may be argumentative/persuasive.

BASIC REQUIREMENTS:

    1) All causes must be in the correct order. (time order)
    2) All causes must relate to the effect.

OTHER ITEMS OF IMPORTANCE:

    1) Adequate connection between the cause and effect must be shown.
    2) Immediate causes should be the focus; ultimate causes are better left out of single paragraphs.
    3) Fallacious reasoning should be avoided. This is the black cat and bad luck sort of thinking.
    4) Avoid complicated procedures for a single paragraph; such topics are better suited for multi-paragraph essays.

METHOD OF CONSTRUCTION:

    1) pick a topic and set it up as a why/how question
    2) answer with causes/reasons
    3) pick best reasons, eliminate fallacious and tenuous ones
    4) arrange the remaining answers logically/natural progression
    5) generate a topic sentence
    6) put forth the reasons in order in the body of the paragraph
    7) write a concluding sentence

WORKING IT THROUGH

1) Let's talk about why someone is successful in school: why Jane does well in school.
2) Now we have to generate some answers: she is smart; she likes to learn; she is studious; she has a good environment to work in; she sets goals; she has a schedule; she is persistent; she wants to do well; she wants to know things; she is willing to sacrifice other things in order to do well at school; her parents are teachers; her older brother has all the tests from when he took her classes.
3) Let's drop the first and last two items; that will make the paragraph fit for more people. Saying she is smart and has teachers for parents eliminates being able to identify with Jane.
4) Here's one possible order: she is inquisitive & wants to know; her home environment is helpful; she sets goals and keeps them, perhaps at a cost; she sets a schedule and follows it; she wants to do well.
5) Generate a topic sentence: Jane does very well in school, but there are reasons why she does.
6) Write out the reasons in order in the body; make good sentences of the items in #4.
7) Write a concluding sentence: Jane does well because she has developed a pattern oriented toward success.

Why Jane Does Well in School

Jane does very well in school, but there are reasons why she does. She is not particularly brilliant, but she does have an inquisitive mind that asks questions and wants to know. In her home she has a strong support group who rewards her efforts and provides opportunities for study time. Jane sets goals for herself that are realistic, and she is willing to sacrifice at times to reach those goals. She establishes a study schedule and sticks to it, especially when it comes to reading, writing reports, and studying for tests. Perhaps most important is that Jane has a great attitude of wanting to excel in whatever she does. Jane does well because she has developed a pattern oriented toward success.

ASSIGNMENT:

Write a cause & effect paragraph composed of seven sentences. The first sentence will be the topic sentence; the five body sentences will briefly review the causes, and the last sentence will provide a conclusion of some sort.

SAMPLE TOPICS: why the X team will/did win the championship, why the rains come each spring, why Saul hated David, why X should/did win the election, why the accident on the freeway happened, why Joe got a bad grade on the test, why Helen's birthday party was a success, why collecting dolls/coins/slot cars is fun, why saving regularly is a good idea, why being obedient to authority is proper. There are really an endless number of topics for this type of paragraph. Remember to keep it simple. Attempting to give the reasons why the United States won World War II could be done in a paragraph, but the reasons would be general and unsubstantiated.

THE COMPARISON PARAGRAPH

A comparison is used to compare two similar ideas or items. Its purpose is to show the topics in relation to one another, often in an attempt to show the superiority of one over the other.

BASIC REQUIREMENTS:

    1) Where possible, comparisons should be in terms of one another.
    2) Contrasts obviously will occur as comparisons are made.

OTHER ITEMS OF IMPORTANCE:

    1) The comparisons should follow an order from least favorable to most favorable or weakest to
        strongest.
    2) Be sure that the two ideas or items have similar characteristics.
    3) Avoid complicated subjects for a single paragraph; such topics are better suited for
        multi-paragraph essays.

METHOD OF CONSTRUCTION:

    1) pick a topic to discuss
    2) find an idea/item for comparison that is similar
    3) brainstorm for the similarities
    4) arrange the order of the points to best suit your purpose
    5) generate a topic sentence
    6) make the comparisons in the body of the paragraph
    7) write a concluding sentence

WORKING IT THROUGH

1) The topic will be authors of Westerns.
2) I will pick two famous authors and compare them.
3) Similarities include style, use of dialogue, use of action, use of character, use of description, true to reality, research put into the work, advertising & promotion, popularity, movement in the story,
4) Set the above in some sort of meaningful order: background & research, dialogue & slang, popularity due to promotion, movement in the story, strong characters.
5) Generate a topic sentence: Some say that Louis L'Amour is more popular today than Zane Grey ever was.
6) Utilize the items in #4 to make comparisons; one comparison per sentence works out well here.
7) Write a concluding sentence: For most readers today, Louis L'Amour is the most popular Western author of all time.

EXAMPLE:

A Choice in Western Authors

Some say that Louis L'Amour is more popular today than Zane Grey ever was. Both authors wrote of the Old West, but L'Amour appears to have done more research while Grey accepted the legends of his time. Zane Grey used much dialect and slang in his writing while L'Amour's writing is more contemporary and easier to follow. One particular factor is that the mass marketing of today has heavily promoted Louis L'Amour whereas Zane Grey did not have such a heavy advertising campaign behind him. Today's reader wants things to happen, and Louis L'Amour's novels are more action packed and move right along while Grey's stories take time to get going. It is hard to remember individual characters from Grey's novels, but the strong characters in L'Amour's novels, especially the Sackett family, do much for his popularity. For most readers today, Louis L'Amour is the most popular Western author of all time.

ASSIGNMENT:

Write a comparison paragraph composed of seven sentences. The first sentence will be the topic sentence; the five body sentences will make the comparisons, and the last sentence will provide a conclusion of some sort.

SAMPLE TOPICS: bees and wasps, thoroughbreds and quarter horses, any two candidates for the same office, two similar brand items such as soaps, cake mixes, or bikes; two people, perhaps authors or poets or politicians or heroes or sports stars, two characters from literature or the Bible, two hymns about a similar idea, two books on a similar subject, the relative merits of two popular cars or engines or TV shows or movies. You get the idea; just pick any two things or people that can be compared for some reason.

SECTION 2

Five Paragraph Essays

ELEMENTS OF A FIVE PARAGRAPH ESSAY

This section of the book is designed to teach you that the typical five paragraph essay has certain parts of it that are quite standard. Once you know what they are, you can utilize them in your own writing. Although some people frown on such a cookbook approach to writing, let me assure you that having a good handle on the organizational principles of a five paragraph composition will be of great benefit to you. Some years ago an article entitled "The Five-Paragraph Essay: An Attempt to Articulate" made a very interesting point. The author, Duane Nichols, cited a study of some 3000 freshman final examination papers from three universities. The interesting fact was that 93% of the A papers had five paragraphs. Essay topics assigned for class themes, final exams, and English proficiency tests seem to naturally call for the following pattern: one paragraph introducing the main idea, a body of three paragraphs explaining the thesis, and a final paragraph concluding the argument.

The introductory and concluding paragraphs require certain elements to be effective and can be quite stylized and still do a good job. The body paragraphs have some general formats they follow as well. You have already gone through the basic seven forms earlier in this book.

The introductory paragraph can be viewed as a funnel or triangle standing on one point. It moves from a general statement to a specific point or purpose. The concluding paragraph somewhat reverses this procedure. The body paragraphs represent the three blocks of the argument. The visual representation of all this is to the right.

The introductory paragraph is designed to introduce the topic, to set the scope and limitation of the paper, to get the reader's attention, to establish the method or approach of the paper, and to give the reason for the paper. If the subject warrants it, some definitions, history and acknowledgments can be made.

The concluding paragraph contains three things: a restatement of the main argument, a summary of the main points, and some generalization about the main idea, usually a judgment or an appeal or a recommended action.

The body paragraphs each contain one main argument or point along with detail that supports that particular point. The body is the detail of the paper. The substance of the paper fills the body paragraphs. The body paragraphs have their own arrangements according to the necessity of the subject matter and the preferences of the writer.

Not all writers follow an organized structure in their writing. In general such writing is poor, but some pieces are strong enough in content and style to still make a positive impression. As a student, I complained to my writing teacher that some famous writer I was reading at the time didn't follow standard writing rules. My teacher's response was something to the effect that I had yet to achieve the famous writer's stature. The message was simple: I needed to learn the techniques and achieve some mastery over them before I could improvise. Of course a certain amount of practice would necessarily precede whatever fame and respect, if any that might ultimately come my way, very little to date I might add. So it is with you, dear student.

Good writing can be learned, at least good principles of organization can be learned. Some folks do have a gift for being able to write, but the rest of us need to put in our time to become proficient at the craft. Learn these techniques, and your writing will improve.

THESIS STATEMENTS

The thesis statement is the most crucial sentence in your entire essay. It is responsible to set the purpose and give a quick road map for the reader at to how the essay will flow. Getting the thesis statement right will not guarantee a good essay, but not having a good thesis statement will surely destroy the probability of having a good essay. The reader needs to know what you are saying and how you are going to deal with the question or subject you have chosen to write on. A good thesis statement gives the reader this information.

A good thesis statement will follow each of these guidelines:

1. **position:** It will come at the end (the last sentence) of the introductory paragraph.

2. **purpose:** It will state the primary purpose of the essay.

3. **format:** It will give a brief overview of the major ideas the essay will present. Each idea in the thesis statement will represent one body paragraph, and the order in which the ideas are mentioned in the thesis statement will be the order of the body paragraphs.

4. **order:** The order of the three items which will be reflected in the three body paragraphs should be logical, suit your argument, and follow normal time & sequence requirements.

5. **parallelism:** The three items should all be expressed with the same grammatical construction.

6. **bias:** It should be written in neutral terms if possible; don't give away your position immediately.

Here is a thesis statement that meets the requirements above: A brief review of potatoes, carrots, and onions will help gardeners to decide whether these crops are valuable additions to their home gardens. Note that it has the three items, all nouns in this case, listed in a particular order. There is no apparent bias in the statement; we don't know whether the items will be recommended or not. The purpose is obvious, a review of the three crops to see if they are good additions to the home garden. The example given is not the only right answer; many variations are possible.

Let's break the above example down a bit. **Position:** this is not covered in the sentence itself. You will learn that in the opening paragraph exercises. **Purpose:** we see the purpose here is to review three crops to see if they are valuable for the home gardener to grow. **Bias:** the thesis does not tell me whether any of these crops are valuable; it simply says we will look at them and decide after the evidence is in. Don't give away your position in the thesis. At the beginning you need to produce the effect of neutrality. Save your bias for the restatement at the end of the essay. This will keep the reader reading, and it gives the effect of your truly being objective since you are letting the facts speak for themselves. **Format:** these are the subject areas under consideration, in this case potatoes, carrots, and onions. **Order:** the order you give for the three ideas or subjects is the order in which you should treat them. Think this through. Among any three points, one will be weaker, and one will be stronger. Generally you want to order your points from weakest to strongest. In the five paragraph essay, each basic point you make will constitute one paragraph. **Parallelism:** in the example thesis statement, I have used three nouns. Not all subjects or ideas can be expressed in a single word. Be careful to keep your three points or ideas in the same grammatical constructions: nouns, verbs, prepositional phrases, verbals, verbal phrases, or whatever suits you just so long as the three items are in parallel structures.

Let's take a typical situation where you are given an assignment, much like those that will follow. Your teacher says to write a short essay on the effects of Columbus discovering the New World. Now, you have to decide a few things. First you can jot down some of the known effects: immigration from Europe, displacement of natives, new trading commodities & new routes, territorial wars with other Europeans and with natives, and so on. Second you will have to decide on some purpose. Perhaps you will try to say the effects were positive or negative. Maybe you will focus on how the common man was affected, or maybe you will generalize but center on how the discovery affected Europe. You see, you do have some choices, so make them carefully.

OK, let's focus on the effects as relating to Spain. Knowing that five paragraphs constitute a short essay, you decide to use the five paragraph format. That means constructing a good thesis sentence, deriving the seven basic sentences from that, and finally more or less filling in the blanks in between.

WORKING IT THROUGH

Purpose: You need to figure out your purpose. Here let's say it is to show the effects of the discovery on Spain were good. The purpose will always reflect your personal bias.

Bias: Now you need to express the purpose without bias.

> We will see if the effects of the discovery of the New World were positive for Spain.

Format: You need to come up with three basic ideas to discuss. Let's talk about increased wealth through trade and force, emigration as an outlet & opportunity, and the problem of wars with the natives and other European states.

Order: Here you need get the three points organized. Since you are going to make the ultimate point that Spain had a positive experience, you will want to go from the least positive to the most positive. Of the three, war is probably the least desirable while wealth is the most positive; that puts emigration in the middle.

Parallelism: You need to express these three points in a similar fashion. Here's a couple of possibilities: war, emigration, and wealth; the problems of war, the benefits of emigration, and the accumulation of wealth.

Now it's time to put it all together. Here's a decent thesis statement.

> We will see if the effects of the discovery of the New World were positive for Spain
> by looking at the results of their wars, emigration, and new wealth.

In review, this thesis statement gives a purpose and an outline to follow while the reader will have to wait for the conclusion to know if the writer thinks it was for the Spain's good or ill.

Again, for emphasis I repeat, the thesis statement is the most important sentence in the five paragraph essay. It isn't the easiest sentence to write, but getting a good thesis statement is really a make or break proposition. Spend time and thought in creating good thesis statements for your own essays. The rewards will be great. What follows are some exercises to give you practice. There are no specific right answers, but some answers will obviously be better than others. Take your time and be thoughtful.

THESIS STATEMENTS #1

DIRECTIONS: Write thesis statements for each of the items below.

1. Your subject is firewood. You will deal with oak, willow, and fir. The end result will be a recommendation about their relative efficiency as a heat source.

2. Success is the subject here. You will explain what it is by giving standard book meanings, explaining some differences between *success* and closely related words, examining some commonly associated ideas and feelings, and reciting an example of success.

3. Your topic here is the causes of floods in Southern Oregon. You will identify three interrelated causes. They are lack of dams, too much rain at once, and warm weather melting the snow pack.

4. Your subject here is how to adequately prepare for an overnight cross country ski trip. You will want to identify three basic stages of preparation. They should include packing for the trip, gathering items from a checklist, and planning on paper to avoid possible problems.

5. This time you will deal with two cars of your choice. You will compare them regarding the appearance, the gas mileage they get, and the general price range, and you will make a judgment regarding which is the best buy in your opinion.

THESIS STATEMENTS #2

DIRECTIONS: Write a thesis statement for each of the following ideas.

1. Write an informative paper on dogs bred for retrieving in water by discussing Labrador, Golden, and Chesapeake Bay Retrievers.

2. Compare any two books of your choice; discuss the plot, the handling of the main character, and the theme of the books.

3. Explain the meaning of *faith* by using the following: a good example, dictionary definitions of the word and its synonyms, and opposite terms and what they mean.

4. Explain the exegesis of a verse of Scripture; review the various steps which include writing a synthesis, explaining hard words, and thoroughly reading the verse.

5. Discuss the relative qualities of Wheaties, Cheerios, and Grape-Nuts. Make a recommendation for purchase.

6. Illustrate what a true Christian is really like by giving examples, citing various verses, and describing typical Christian actions.

7. From two hymns of your choice, tell which is best on the basis of the words, the music, and the extent to which it glorifies God.

8. Compare the relative merits of Rook, Shanghai, and Hearts as card games.

9. Describe the process of proper studying for a chapter test in history; discuss making an outline, defining important words, reading the text, and reviewing your personal notes.

10. Determine the relative merits of investing in gold, silver, and copper.

THESIS STATEMENTS #3

DIRECTIONS: Write a thesis statement for each of the following ideas. The information given below will be more general in nature, more like what will happen in some of your other classes. You will need to come up with the three points and the position yourself.

1. Compare two contemporary novelists.

2. Discuss the causes of the energy crisis.

3. Should salmon be on the endangered species list?

4. Make a case regarding the creation theory of the universe.

5. Write a short paper on the historical treatment of Indians in America.

6. Attack or defend the lottery.

7. Did the United States do right in turning the Panama Canal over to Panama?

8. Make a case for or against SUV's.

9. Write a short paper on immigration to the US during the 1800's.

10. Evaluate nuclear power.

INTRODUCTORY PARAGRAPHS

The introductory paragraph can be very stylized and still be effective. A simple method for writing the introductory paragraph follows: keep these rules in mind.

1. The ideas expressed will go from very general at the beginning to very specific at the end.

2. The first sentence should catch the reader's attention and point him in the direction of the main subject. It could contain a statistic, quote, question, or reminder.

3. The thesis statement will be the last sentence in the introductory paragraph.

4. The thesis statement should contain the three[1] subtopics which will be used as the paragraph topics in the body. The order of the subtopics should be the same for both the thesis statement and the three body paragraphs.

5. The thesis statement states the fundamental point that you are trying to make in the essay.

[1]In this case we have used three subtopics because you will have three paragraphs in the bodies of your five paragraph essays that will come later in this book. In practice, the number of paragraphs in a short essay will vary, but three is a very good number for very good reasons.

INTRODUCTORY PARAGRAPH EXAMPLE

Animals have always been a part of man's life. Many animals have been domesticated for man's use down through history. Most of the domestic animals are found on farms. Cattle are one of the most widely found farm animals for various reasons. Let's see if the traditional cow is still valuable today by looking at such products as leather, meat, and milk.

Note how the categories in the above example get more specific with each sentence. The categories go from *animals* to *farm animals* to *cattle*. In the thesis statement, the three specific topics are *leather, meat*, and *milk*. Think of the categories as ever shrinking boxes. The largest category is animals. Within the box of animals, there is a smaller box, domestic animals, and within that box we find yet a smaller box, farm animals. Finally within that last box, we have cattle. Obviously we could have even smaller boxes within the cattle box; we could have cattle kept for milk, cattle kept for beef, various breeds, and so forth.

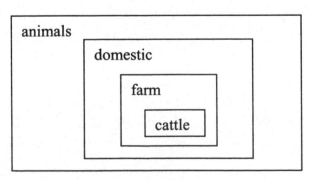

WORKING IT THROUGH

Let's say you have to write a short paper on pizza. You first have to decide on your thesis sentence. Having decided that, you have the last sentence of your introductory paragraph. Let's use the sentence below for our thesis statement regarding pizza.

> By reviewing preparation, variety, and availability, we will see if pizza has become a favorite American food.

Note the three subtopics in the above thesis: **preparation**, **variety**, and **availability**.

Now it is time to create the introductory paragraph.

Step 1: Brainstorm for some ever reducing categories. For this example we will use the categories below.

> food   Italian food   fast food   pizza

Step 2: Think of some catchy introductory statement regarding the most general category.

> The variety of food available to man means everyone should find some foods he or she likes to eat.

Step 3: Create a sentence for each of the smaller categories. Remember these sentences have to flow and point to the thesis statement.

Italian food	Of the many ethnic varieties of food available, Italian food is one the more popular types found in the United States.
fast food	Italian foods can be divided into fast foods and traditional meals.
pizza	Pizza is probably the best known of the Italian fast foods.

Step 4. Now all you have to do is tack on the attention getter at the front and the thesis at the end, and you will have your introductory paragraph.

> The variety of food available to man means everyone should find some foods he or she likes to eat. Of the many ethnic varieties of food available, Italian food is one the more popular types found in the United States. Italian foods can be divided into fast foods and traditional meals. Pizza is probably the best known of the Italian fast foods. By reviewing preparation, variety, and availability, we will see if pizza has become a favorite American food.

INTRODUCTORY PARAGRAPH PRACTICE #1

Your job is to write an introductory paragraph for one of the subjects below. You should also list the categories used in order from general to specific and list the three specific subtopics in your thesis statement.

SUBJECTS: 1) personal computer, 2) hair dryer, 3) Jeep 4x4 pickup, 4) Labrador retriever,

CATEGORIES: _____, _____, _____

SUBTOPICS: _____, _____, _____

INTRODUCTORY PARAGRAPH PRACTICE #2

DIRECTIONS: Treat each item below as the subject of a paper. Your job is to structure the introductory paragraph. For each item identify the three general categories and the three specific topics to be included in the thesis statement. You are to structure all five. Then pick one of the five and write an introductory paragraph based on your structure.

1. George Washington

CATEGORIES: _____, _____, _____

SUBTOPICS: _____, _____, _____

2. recent US Presidents

CATEGORIES: _____, _____, _____

SUBTOPICS: _____, _____, _____

3. sports cars

CATEGORIES: _____, _____, _____

SUBTOPICS: _____, _____, _____

4. Romans chapter 9

CATEGORIES: _____, _____, _____

SUBTOPICS: _____, _____, _____

5. Monopoly (the game)

CATEGORIES: _____, _____, _____

SUBTOPICS: _____, _____, _____

INTRODUCTORY PARAGRAPH PRACTICE #3

DIRECTIONS: Treat each item below as the subject of a paper. Your job is to structure the introductory paragraph. For each item identify the three general categories and the three specific subtopics to be included in the thesis statement. You are to structure all five. Then pick one of the five and write an introductory paragraph based on your structure.

1. Abraham Lincoln

CATEGORIES: _____, _____, _____

SUBTOPICS: _____, _____, _____

2. recent top movies

CATEGORIES: _____, _____, _____

SUBTOPICS: _____, _____, _____

3. collector hobbies

CATEGORIES: _____, _____, _____

SUBTOPICS: _____, _____, _____

4. Thou shalt not kill!

CATEGORIES: _____, _____, _____

SUBTOPICS: _____, _____, _____

5. card games

CATEGORIES: _____, _____, _____

SUBTOPICS: _____, _____, _____

CONCLUDING PARAGRAPHS

The concluding paragraph is usually composed in a standard format no matter what kind of expository essay has been written. A simple method for writing concluding paragraphs follows.

1. The first sentence should restate the thesis; it should be reworded to avoid repetition. It should contain both the main point or purpose and the three main subtopics.

2. The next three sentences should summarize the information from the body paragraphs and make conclusions regarding them. Each sentence should deal with one major subtopic, preferably in the order that they occur.

3. The final sentence should be some type of thought-provoking generalization about the subject.

CONCLUDING PARAGRAPH EXAMPLE

Thus it can be seen that the traditional cow is still valuable since it fulfills a variety of man's needs such as leather, meat, and milk. Most real leather still comes from cattle. Beef, the meat of cows, is the principal meat on the market in the United States today. The dairy cow accounts for 95% of all the milk consumed by man. Today the cow is almost as necessary to man's existence as it was hundreds of years ago.

From the above example we can note a number of things. The first sentence restates the purpose, *is still valuable*, and gives the subtopics, *leather, meat*, and *milk*. The next three sentences each summarize one subtopic. The final statement generalizes about the cow and its uses; it justifies or re-emphasizes the purpose in a final way.

☞ 1st sentence = restatement of thesis
☞ 2nd sentence = summary statement of subtopic #1
☞ 3rd sentence = summary statement of subtopic #2
☞ 4th sentence = summary statement of subtopic #3
☞ 5th sentence = general statement of purpose

WORKING IT THROUGH

Let's go back to the topic of pizza and use the introductory paragraph to structure a concluding paragraph.

Step 1: Restate the thesis in a positive way.

After looking at preparation, variety, and availability, it is evident that pizza is now a favorite American food.

Step 2: Write a summary statement regarding each subtopic in order.

The ease of preparation makes pizza a favorite for cooks and non-cooks.
Since pizza comes in so many varieties, there is something for almost everyone.
The wide availability of pizza is a testimony to its popularity.

Step 3: Write a final sentence that further makes your point or summarizes in some way your entire argument.

Why not have some pizza this week and become a part of a popular new American food tradition?

Put them all together, and you have your concluding paragraph. Once you really grasp the simplicity of this method, you will see that the concluding paragraph pretty much writes itself.

After looking at preparation, variety, and availability, it is evident that pizza is now a favorite American food. The ease of preparation makes pizza a favorite for cooks and non-cooks. Since pizza comes in so many varieties, there is something for almost everyone. The wide availability of pizza is a testimony to its popularity. Why not have some pizza this week and become a part of a popular new American food tradition?

CONCLUDING PARAGRAPH PRACTICE #1

DIRECTIONS: Your job is to write a concluding paragraph based on one of the following items. Remember, you will need a thesis statement to do this, but hopefully you will find one you have already created back on the first thesis statement exercise.

1. wood fuel efficiency found in willow, oak, and fir

2. floods from related causes of lack of dams, heavy rains, and melting snow

3. good trip preparation utilizing planning, check listing, and packing

CONCLUDING PARAGRAPH PRACTICE #2

The concluding paragraph is usually composed in a standard format no matter what kind of expository essay has been written. We would say that it is highly stylized but effective.

1st sentence = restatement of thesis
2nd sentence = summary statement of subtopic #1
3rd sentence = summary statement of subtopic #2
4th sentence = summary statement of subtopic #3
5th sentence = general statement of purpose

CONCLUDING PARAGRAPH EXAMPLE

THESIS: By checking the plot, characters, and special effects, it can be seen if the "Lone Ranger" is a good radio program.

CONCLUDING PARAGRAPH: It can now be concluded that the "Lone Ranger" is a good radio program based on its plot, characters, and special effects. The plots are fast paced, suspenseful, and interesting. The characters although quite typical of westerns are still creative and believable. The special effects are handled well and enhance the program in many ways. The "Lone Ranger" is worthy of anyone's attention who enjoys a good old time radio drama.

DIRECTIONS: Using the above as an example and guide, your job is to write a concluding paragraph for one of the following thesis statements.

1) To see if Wheaties is a good breakfast, we will look at its food value, cost per serving, and ease of preparation.

2) By comparing the total sales figures, annual costs of maintenance, and trade-in values, it can be shown which is the better deal, a Toyota or Nissan pickup.

3) Determining the proper procedure for making fudge brownies involves gathering the necessary ingredients and utensils, making and baking the mixture, and cleaning up.

CONCLUDING PARAGRAPH PRACTICE #3

This is exercise is just like the one found on the previous page. Look there for the example and the outline of the concluding paragraph. Remember, when your concluding paragraphs follow the formula, they won't be original in format, but they will be effective in summing up the material and will provide good endings for your upcoming essays. The concluding paragraph formula works, so use it and profit from it.

DIRECTIONS: Using the example found on page 29 as a guide, your job is to write a concluding paragraph for one of the following thesis statements.

1) To see if raising our own chickens is profitable, we must consider egg production, meat production, and feed and labor costs.

2) By comparing the total sales figures, initial cost of equipment, and available software, the best buy between computer A and computer B (name your choices) can be determined.

3) Deciding the ideal vacation for a family of four involves gathering the information, figuring costs, and holding family councils.

TRANSITIONS

The function of transitions is to guide the reader from point to point smoothly. For the most part in this book we are interested in proper paragraph transitions. From sentence to sentence within a paragraph, the general flow of the content is generally sufficient, but paragraphs represent a break in thought to a related but new subject.

Transitions are accomplished in two major ways: reference and connectives. Both can also be used together.

REFERENCE

When using reference as a transition method, it usually involves the last sentence of the leading paragraph and the first sentence of the following paragraph. A specific item is repeated, referred to synonymously, or referred to by a pronoun. You will note that reference transition is quite easy from the thesis statement at the end of the introductory paragraph to the topic sentence of the first body paragraph since the thesis gives an outline of the three subjects or areas to be covered, and the topic sentence introduces the first of those topics.

CONNECTIVES

Connectives are words or phrases that usually appear in the first sentence of the following paragraph. They signal some type of change or shift. Overuse of certain connectives results in some awkwardness so be careful. Examples of various types of connectives appear below.

time/spatial relationships: *soon, next, then, later, finally, eventually, first, second, ..., now, meanwhile, afterward, since, nearby, above, below, in front (back), to the right (left)*

sequence: *in addition, also, furthermore, moreover, another, likewise, next, similarly, finally, besides, again, first of all, secondly*

contrast: *but, on the other hand, however, rather, nevertheless, otherwise, yet, still, in spite of*

results: *therefore, hence, because, thus, consequently, as a result, for, so, accordingly*

examples following: *for instance, an example being, for example, take the case of, in other words*

Think of transitions as road signs that indicate which direction an argument or discussion is about to take. Transitions should map out your logic so that your thoughts can easily be followed by the reader. It is important to use the transitions correctly; don't send false signals. The words in the three lists below all serve specific purposes; *pro* words are used for introducing favorable ideas; *con* words are used with negatives.

PRO		CON		CONCLUSION	
of course	conceivably	not at all	on the contrary	therefore	in short
no doubt	perhaps	however	yet	all in all	thus
doubtless	although	nevertheless	surely	and so	so
to be sure	though	but	notwithstanding	finally	in other words
granted	whereas	furthermore	no	hence	consequently
granted that	certainly	indeed	still	on the whole	

BODY PARAGRAPH CONSTRUCTION

GENERAL COMMENTS:

1. The first sentence in a body paragraph is the topic sentence of that paragraph. It states the general topic to be discussed in that paragraph. In the five paragraph essay, the topic sentence will contain one of the three subtopics mentioned in the thesis statement.

2. Transitions occur in one of two places in the body paragraph. The transition can come in the topic sentence, or it can be in the final sentence of the body paragraph. Transitions show the reader that the focus of attention is being shifted.

3. The secondary sentences in a body paragraph will be subordinate to the topic sentence. For instance, the secondary sentences may be examples of the main topic, parts of a process falling under a general heading, or facts supporting a given position. Additionally, the order of the secondary sentences should be logical. The weakest point should be first with the best or strongest point being last.

4. All the body paragraphs should be similar in length to one another. No one paragraph should be markedly shorter or longer than its mates. This is called balance.

THESIS: To see if having a vegetable garden is worthwhile, it would be valuable to look at the benefits of homegrown potatoes, tomatoes, and corn.

3rd BODY PARAGRAPH: The final vegetable under consideration here is corn. Homegrown corn can come in many varieties that are not available commercially. Garden corn provides stalks for animal fodder and for decoration. Corn grown in one's own garden can be harvested over a long period if the plantings are staggered. The best reason for homegrown corn is the freshness since it can be harvested just before eating for maximum tenderness and sweetness.

NOTE: A transition, *final*, appears in the topic sentence. The topic sentence identifies *corn* as the subject of the paragraph. Each of the other four sentences brings out a positive fact about garden corn. The best fact in the author's mind is saved for last to provide the greatest impact on the reader.

You will write many body paragraphs when writing your five paragraph essays. The content and organization of those body paragraphs will be influenced by both your topic and the overall format of the five paragraph essay.

BODY PARAGRAPH EXERCISE #1

YOUR JOB: Create one body paragraph from the following thesis statement. Be sure to have a topic sentence with a transition and to have four or five secondary sentences making your point. Only do one body paragraph; please identify if it is the first, second, or third body paragraph.

THESIS: By checking the plots, characters, and special effects, it can be seen if the "Lone Ranger" is a good radio program.

SEVEN SENTENCE SKELETON

There are seven sentences which form the skeleton of a five paragraph essay. Of these seven, six of them relate to the most basic sentence of all, the thesis statement. Thus, the thesis statement is the sentence that should be decided upon first. Since the thesis statement provides the basis for the other main sentences, care and effort should be exercised when creating it. A good thesis will generally yield a good essay.

Think of the thesis as the backbone, the other six kernel sentences as the rest of the bones, and the bulk of the sentences in the essay as muscle tissue. Remember, it is best to build on a solid foundation.

Here are the seven sentences in order of their appearance.

> eye catcher (the introductory sentence, first sentence in the first paragraph)
> thesis statement (last sentence in the first paragraph, most important sentence in essay)
> topic sentence BP #1 (first sentence in the second paragraph)
> topic sentence BP #2 (first sentence in the third paragraph)
> topic sentence BP #3 (first sentence in the fourth paragraph)
> thesis restatement (first sentence of last paragraph)
> close/final statement (last sentence of last paragraph, your parting shot)

The seven sentences are not written in their final order of appearance. The thesis statement is the first sentence to be written; then the three topic sentences for the body paragraphs and the restatement can be written. The concluding statement and the introductory statement are written last.

WORKING IT THROUGH

Here's an example. We'll take the "Lone Ranger" radio program as our subject and talk about the plot, the characters, and the special effects. Our first job is to write the thesis.

> By checking the plot, characters, and special effects, it can be seen if the "Lone Ranger" is a good radio program.

Now we need to write the three topic sentences for the body paragraphs. The first BP subtopic is plot; the second is characters, and the third is special effects.

> Plot is important in radio drama.
> A second area of concern is how well the characters are developed.
> Finally, special effects have a great deal to do with how a radio program is received.

The rewrite of the thesis statement needs to be positive and affirming of the position of the writer.

> It can now be concluded that the "Lone Ranger" is a good radio program based on its plot, characters, and special effects.

Finally we can write the concluding and the introductory sentences.

> The "Lone Ranger" is worthy of anyone's attention who enjoys a good old time radio drama.
> Radio is a unique means of presenting drama.

Having written all seven of the sentences, let's put them in their order of occurrence.

> Radio is a unique means of presenting drama.
> By checking the plot, characters, and special effects, it can be seen if the "Lone Ranger" is a good radio program.
> Plot is important in radio drama.
> A second area of concern is how well the characters are developed.
> Finally, special effects have a great deal to do with how a radio program is received.
> It can now be concluded that the "Lone Ranger" is a good radio program based on its plot, characters, and special effects.
> The "Lone Ranger" is worthy of anyone's attention who enjoys a good old time radio drama.

From the above, you can see the essential skeleton of a five paragraph essay. The first two sentences will open and close the introductory paragraph. We see a movement from general to specific. In the thesis we see both purpose and a brief outline of coverage. Getting a good thesis statement is essential. The other six sentences are quite dependent on the thesis. The three topic sentences for the body paragraphs simply introduce the ideas put forth in the thesis. Here we have plot, character, and special effects. The last two sentences open and close the final paragraph. The skeleton provides the framework on which to hang the other details we might wish to include.

I urge you to catch the vision of the power of this type of outline for a five paragraph essay. You will find it most helpful in making your writing flow in a logical fashion. Yes, it takes some time initially to figure this sort of thing out, but once the seven sentences are written, the rest should come quite easily.

SEVEN SENTENCE EXERCISE #1

Directions: Create the thesis statement first, then write the other six sentences. This will provide the outline. Do not write the full essay.

TOPIC INFORMATION: prove, compare, or recommend something about Cornish Cross, White Leghorn, and Plymouth Rock chickens.

eye catcher:

thesis statement:

topic sentence BP #1:

topic sentence BP #2:

topic sentence BP #3:

thesis restatement:

close/final statement:

FIVE PARAGRAPH ESSAYS

This next portion of the book is composed of the seven basic formats for organizing the body paragraphs of a typical five paragraph essay. You will recognize the formats as being the same as the single paragraph formats. The order of magnitude is raised a level, but the methodology is very similar.

A set of general guidelines is given on the next page. These are applicable to all of the seven formats. Most of the information given is review from what you have learned when studying the previous section on the elements of a five paragraph essay. The general guidelines sheet simply puts it all in one place for easy access. Something that you can do for yourself is to use the guidelines sheet as a basis for creating your own check sheet. Make up a check sheet on a grid basis so that you can use it over and over again. For each essay, systematically go through it before you turn it in and check off the items that you have completed. Your teacher may require this of you anyway.

The seven examples are laid out for you on two pages each. A general statement about the format and its common uses is made. Then some particular points are given. Next you will find a series of steps that are a how to do it scenario for the particular format you are dealing with. Many of the steps repeat from format to format, but there are differences. Finally each step is outlined with a particular subject used as an example. You should find this to be helpful. After the first type, you will even get a seven sentence outline for each of the formats.

You can expect to write at least one essay of each type, but you may be required to write more. That is up to your teacher. Take a look at the five paragraph report check sheet at the back of this book. It or something quite similar to it will be the evaluation tool for your essays. Knowing what is expected of you will enable you to produce a better end product.

Permit me a small story here. At one point I taught a fellow English teacher how to explain these formats to his students. We were both teaching high school sophomores in the same school, and the classes were to be somewhat similar in content. He went through the year teaching pretty much from the notes I gave him. The next fall before school we were chatting, and he mentioned that he had gone to Hawaii for the summer and taken some classes at the university there. He remarked that he had gotten the only "A" in an advanced writing class and that he had done it by simply using the formulas that he had learned and taught his sophomores the previous year. The point is that these formats work. If you will learn them and use them, you will have a decided edge on others when it comes to writing.

A well-organized piece of writing is effective; it makes its point. Good, tight organization lends credibility to the argument because the progression of the ideas is both logical and rational. The argument seems to make sense because it is definitive and organized. You, the writer come across as understanding the subject well; the writing carries an aura of expertise because it is clear. All of these impressions work on the reader to your advantage when you present an organized argument. Cogent writing makes a positive impression; it is believable. Use these formats to aid your writing to be more effective.

FIVE PARAGRAPH ESSAYS: GENERAL GUIDELINES

1. All essays will have five paragraphs which will consist of the following: one introductory paragraph, three body paragraphs, and one concluding paragraph.

2. All paragraphs should be roughly the same in length. This is part of what is meant by *balance*.

3. The introductory paragraph must start with a catchy first sentence which relates in general to the main subject. This sentence is designed to get the reader's interest. Short quotes, rhetorical questions, and startling statistics are often used in the first sentence. Although it comes first, it is best written later in the process.

4. The introductory paragraph must have a thesis statement as its last sentence. The thesis statement has two functions: a) to identify the purpose and specific topic of the essay and b) to give the outline of the three main points which will be discussed in the three body paragraphs.

5. The interim sentences in the introductory paragraph should become narrower in scope and point toward the thesis statement. These sentences may give needed background and definitions needed to understand the essay.

6. The body paragraphs must each contain a topic sentence as the first sentence of that paragraph. All topic sentences should reflect one of the three main points stated in the thesis statement. Also, the three points should occur in the order mentioned in the thesis statement. The order should be logical and beneficial to the argument presented in the thesis.

7. Each body paragraph should have the topic sentence and about four or five sentences with a new supporting detail in each sentence.

8. Whenever possible, the organization of each body paragraph should be similar to that of the other body paragraphs.

9. Transitions need to be included in each body paragraph to maintain continuity. The transition usually occurs in the topic sentences.

10. The first sentence of concluding paragraph should be a restatement of the thesis statement, but it should be definite and state the unequivocal position of the paper.

11. The next three sentences of the concluding paragraph should summarize in order the information contained in the three body paragraphs.

12. The final sentence of the concluding paragraph should contain an appeal, recommendation, or application of the position taken by the paper.

GENERAL GUIDELINES TO TOPIC SELECTION

1. You should be interested in the topic, and it should hold some casual interest for others; you need to raise that interest level if possible.

2. You should have some knowledge of the topic; it is easiest to write about what you know. Additional information can always be looked up.

3. The reader of your paper should gain something: information, opinion, and even pleasure.

THE EXAMPLE ESSAY

A common method for organizing a five paragraph essay is to build the three body paragraphs around three examples where each body paragraph focuses on one of the examples. The examples are useful for illustration and comparison.

A. Example essays give three major examples of the subject defined in the thesis statement. Generally the purpose is to illustrate a point by giving three examples.

B. The typical information found in each body paragraph will be details about the specific example chosen.

C. The examples can be from best to worst or weakest to strongest, but an order of some sort should be evident. Putting the best or strongest example last is helpful when making a positive point; the reverse would hold true for making a negative point.

D. One nice thing about example essays is that the body paragraphs can all be organized the same way. For instance, the topic sentence identifies the specific example; the next three or four sentences could give different types of data, appearance, composition, volume, heat factors, weight, whatever categories you picked. The final sentence may include your personal view or stated preference. All body paragraphs would have similar information formatted in the same manner.

Here is a general procedure for constructing an example essay.

1) Determine the general topic area.
2) Brainstorm for examples; put down all things that come to mind.
3) Sort and eliminate examples while narrowing the topic focus.
4) Determine the thesis statement.
5) Arrange examples in order best suited for topic and purpose.
6) Develop suitable sub-points and details for each example.
7) Fill in the outline.
8) Create the seven sentence skeleton.
9) Write the rough draft.

WORKING IT THROUGH

1) We decide our general topic area. For our purposes, we will talk about root crops in home gardens.

2) Next we list various root crops such as radishes, onions, potatoes, garlic, leeks, carrots, turnips, parsnips, peanuts, and whatever else comes to mind.

3) Reviewing the list we see there are many to choose from, so we might pick some that are most common such as carrots, potatoes and onions. We might narrow the focus to alliums and pick leeks, garlic and onions. There are numerous options when narrowing the focus and picking the items needed. The point is to sense some specific direction for the essay and to choose those examples best suited for your purpose from the list.

4) Now we need to write a the thesis: Most gardeners should consider potatoes, carrots and onions as probable crops for their home gardens.

5) In essence, this step is really simultaneous with the last one. The order of the examples in the thesis sentence needs to be consistent with the purpose of the thesis, so determining the order occurs when establishing the thesis statement. Of course, after all details are uncovered, the order may be rearranged if necessary.

6) Again we seek categories which have something in common for discussion within the various examples. In this case we might comment about appearance, planting conditions and requirements, storage capabilities, harvest period, and ultimate uses of each crop. Once the categories are selected, they must be ordered in the best fashion to make the thesis point.

7) Having determined the categories and ordered them to best advantage, the next operation is to fill in the actual details for each example. For instance, we might describe the physical appearance of the potato as brown, red, or white, generally spherical in shape with knobs or lumps, and varying in size from that of a golf ball to softball. We would then fill in the details for the rest of the potato categories and then do likewise with the others. A sample outline follows.

BP#1 - potatoes   Topic sentence with transition
 a) brown, red, white - ball shaped, lumpy - golf ball size & up
 b) plant sets in spring - trench, tower, mulch - space eater
 c) cold storage, root cellar, fairly good keeper
 d) main vegetable, soups, stews

BP#2 - carrots   Topic sentence with transition
 a) orange - cylindrical, often tapered, 2"-12" long
 b) seed in spring or fall - must keep moist - deep soil
 c) mulch over in ground, root cellar
 d) raw, soups, stews, salads, main vegetable

BP#3 - onions   Topic sentence with transition
 a) white, red, yellow - ball shaped - slim green to softball size
 b) spring seeding or sets - loose ground - deep or shallow
 c) dried & hung in cool, dry place
 d) salads, soups, stews, raw

8) Using the seven sentence technique, the skeleton of the essay can now be framed.

intro:	Do you know which two hobbies are most popular with Americans today?
thesis:	Most gardeners should consider potatoes, carrots and onions as probable crops for their home gardens.
1st BP:	Potatoes are a useful crop for most home gardeners to grow.
2nd BP:	Another crop, carrots, is quite often found in home gardens.
3rd BP:	Finally, home grown onions are popular in many home vegetable gardens.
restatement:	Having seen the benefits of potatoes, carrots, and onions, it is reasonable to say you will find them in most home gardens.
final:	If you make space for these three crops when you plant your garden this year, you will be like most other gardeners.

9) The body paragraphs can now be fleshed out, and the introductory and concluding paragraphs can be devised and put into place. After creating the rough draft, proof read for mechanical errors and general flow of the presentation and make the necessary changes. Here's an example.

Root Crops in the Home Garden

Do you know which two hobbies are most popular with Americans today? The answer is reading and gardening. Gardening includes flowers, vegetables, and all kinds of other plantings. Vegetable gardens are found in all sections of the country and even in major cities. Root crops are a traditional part of the vegetable garden. Most gardeners should consider potatoes, carrots and onions as probable crops for their home gardens.

Potatoes are a useful crop for most home gardeners to grow. In size, potatoes should be at least the size of a golf ball; from there they can range up to a pound or better. They are lumpy but roughly ball or oblong shaped and come in red, brown, white, yellow, and even purple colors. Potatoes are commonly planted from sets in the early spring. They keep fairly well in cold storage after harvest, so you can enjoy them for quite some time. Potatoes are useful as a main vegetable, and they are often found in soups and stews.

Another crop, carrots, is quite often found in home gardens. Carrots are generally orange and cylindrical in shape tapering toward the bottom. They range in length from two to over twelve inches. They are seeded in the spring or the fall, but the ground needs to be kept moist for them to germinate. Carrots are good keepers in storage and in some conditions can be kept right in the ground. Carrots have many uses in a meal; they can be a side vegetable, but more often they are found in soups, stews, and salads, or they may be eaten raw as an appetizer.

Finally, home grown onions are popular in many home vegetable gardens. They come in red, white, or yellow varieties and are generally ball shaped. Green onions are young onions not fully developed; when developed, onions may be from golf ball to softball size. Onions can be planted by seed or by sets, and they need loose ground. After harvest they can keep for quite a while if dried properly and hung in a cool and dry place. A few people like raw onions, but mostly they find their way into salads, soups, and stews.

Having seen the benefits of potatoes, carrots, and onions, it is reasonable to say you will find them in most home gardens. Potatoes are a mainstay for many meals, and they are popular and easy to grow. Carrots are found in most vegetable gardens since they have so many uses. Onions are also quite useful in a variety of meals and are therefore a regular favorite with home gardeners. If you make space for these three crops when you plant your garden this year, you will be like most other gardeners.

THE CLASSIFICATION ESSAY

The function of the classification essay is to place an idea or concept into a framework of similar ideas or concepts. Classifying means placing the topic along with others in its class. The reader is then able to assign a similar set of ideas to the topic. Once a person knows where an idea fits in, a number of associated ideas can then be assigned to it.

    A. Classification essays illustrate three major categories of the subject as defined in the thesis statement. Generally the purpose is to make some point by classifying the subject.

    B. The three major categories or subdivisions should be of similar or equal value in importance and should be clear and familiar.

    C. Each category should in some way help illustrate the thesis. The individual body paragraphs will be filled with information about and sub classifications of the general category of the paragraph.

    D. Stereotyping is an example of overuse of classification and should be avoided.

Here is a general procedure for constructing a classification essay.

1) Pick a topic to classify & the point to be made.
2) Brainstorm for categories/subdivisions.
3) Arrange categories in order of probable use.
4) Determine specific thesis statement.
5) Develop suitable subdivisions and details for each main category.
6) Set up the seven sentence skeleton.
7) Write the rough draft.

WORKING IT THROUGH

1) We decide our general topic area. For this illustration, we will talk about bows. Our point will be their popularity today.

2) Next we list various categories or subdivisions about bows: styles, history, use, materials, design, brands, accessories, and whatever else comes to mind.

3) In order to show the continuity of the bow and its popularity, we might have a general breakdown as follows: historical design, styles & use; modern brands, designs and uses; popular accessories, clubs, meets today. The point is to sense some specific direction for the essay and to choose those categories best suited to illustrate our purpose.

4) The thesis we will use follows: A brief review of the bow's historical development, modern designs, and available accessories will reveal its continued popularity even today.

5) Now we can list out the categories per paragraph that we might use.

Body paragraph #1 deals with history. We have a number of things to discuss here: ancient uses, designs, and materials come to mind.

BP #2 is about modern bows. Here again we can talk about modern design and materials in particular. Certain other information about modern bows might be included. In fact, the organization of the two paragraphs should be quite similar.

BP #3 will focus on accessories and what's available today to strengthen the idea that popularity creates its own demand.

6) Using the seven sentence technique, the skeleton of the essay can now be framed.

intro:	Only a few ancient tools have been continually redesigned and utilized throughout history.
thesis:	A brief review of the bow's historical development, modern designs, and available accessories will reveal its popularity even today.
1st BP:	All down through history the bow has proved to be useful in many cultures even though its design and composition has been varied.
2nd BP:	Today's bows are quite sophisticated in design and are made of many high tech materials.
3rd BP:	The wealth of accessories for bows today attests to the overall popularity of the bow itself.
restatement:	Once the weapon of choice in battle and the hunt, the bow today still commands great respect and favor as witnessed by the multiple modern designs and high availability of secondary products associated with it.
final:	Take another look at the bow and arrow; you just may find it to be a pleasurable recreational experience for you and your family.

7) The body paragraphs can now be fleshed out with details; the introductory and concluding paragraphs can be devised and put into place. After creating the rough draft, proof read for mechanical errors and general flow of the presentation and make the necessary changes. Please find a sample on the next page.

The Ageless Popularity of the Bow

Only a few ancient tools have been continually redesigned and utilized throughout history. Those tools which have survived in some form or another have been both useful and popular. One such set of tools we could classify as weapons. Personal weapons can also have practical uses other than defense. The bow is one of these tools that has survived. A brief review of the bow's historical development, modern designs, and available accessories will reveal its popularity even today.

All down through history the bow has proved to be useful in many cultures even though its design and composition has been varied. Original bows were made of wood or horn or some combination of the two materials. The size of the bow was determined by its use. The Mongols had a very short bow to be used from the back of a horse while the English developed the long bow, which was shot by a man standing on the ground. Bows have been used for the taking of game as well as in war. The popularity of the bow is seen by its place in many different times and cultures.

Today's bows are quite sophisticated in design and are made of many high tech materials. We now have designs that were unheard of a hundred years ago. Manufacturers produce regular bows, reflex bows, recurve bows, and compound bows. Today most bows are made of some combination of materials. Wood may or may not be part of a bow; the high tech laminates of plastics and metals and woods and glass make for a dazzling array of possible combinations. The very diverse selection of bows available today attests to their continuing popularity.

The wealth of accessories for bows today attests to the overall popularity of the bow itself. A quick look at a hunting and fishing catalog will give you some ideas. You can find bow sights and bow releases along with all sorts of things to wear and use when either target shooting or hunting. Even reels and line and special arrows are available for fishing with a bow. Quivers have changed to where now the popular style holds a very few arrows and is mounted on the bow itself.

Once the weapon of choice in battle and the hunt, the bow today still commands great respect and favor as witnessed by the multiple modern designs and high availability of secondary products associated with it. In the world of history, the bow is found as a integral in almost all cultures and geographies. Today, the shear variety of bows available speaks to its popularity as a sporting tool. Add to that the generous number of bow accessories currently available, and you will find the bow is widely popular today. Take another look at the bow and arrow; you just may find it to be a pleasurable recreational experience for you and your family.

THE DEFINITION ESSAY

Building a five paragraph essay by defining a term can be very effective. The three body paragraphs form the core of the definition and are divided up according in varying ways. The function of an essay by definition is to present an understanding of an abstract term so that the reader will have a clear idea of what is meant by the term.

A. Definition essays define a term or idea in a variety of ways. The general organization is reflected in the thesis statement. The purpose is to give a clear understanding of the term or idea.

B. The information found in each body paragraph will vary according to the type of definition utilized in each paragraph.

C. The usual manner of procedure is to begin with lexical type definitions and move on to other methods. No particular order is better or worse than another in the arrangement of the second and third body paragraphs and the details within them.

D. Words used out of context are underlined or italicized. For example, the word *little* in this sentence is used as a word out of context.

E. Immediately below are some types of definitions that can be used in the body paragraphs.
   1) dictionary definitions and synonyms
   2) closely associated words and their differences
   3) function: what it is, does, how/why it is used
   4) connotations: associated meanings and feelings
   5) logical definition: place with others in its class and explain how it differs
   6) extended definition: history of the term & its use, examples of items or
      situations or experiences, analogies and comparisons, exclusion by
      showing what it is not but perhaps thought to be, and opposition by
      showing the exact opposite

Here is a general procedure for constructing a definition essay.

1) Determine the term or idea to define.
2) Gather applicable information regarding the six items above.
3) Arrange the order of the points you will use.
4) Write a thesis statement
5) Set up the seven sentence skeleton.
6) Flesh out the various segments of the definition.
7) Write the rough draft.

1) We decide our general topic area. For our purposes, we will talk about faith.
2) Next we gather information. *faith = belief, religion, trust, loyalty*
   faith: complete trust or confidence, unquestioning belief in
   "Now faith is the substance of things hoped for, the evidence of things not seen."
         Heb 11:1
   faith brings assurance & stability to life, used by many to cope with the difficulties &
         circumstances of life, gives direction
   associated ideas = happiness, assurance, being right, safety, comfort
   blind obedience - differs re depth, thoughtfulness, rationale
   from Latin *fidere* - to trust
   examples of: Scripture - Abraham, David, Noah – in life: astronauts going into space, Columbus
   likened unto a boat - placed within on the seas of life
   not just a shell of duties/laws but guidelines for growth & direction
   opposite of *mistrust, doubt, unbelief*

3) Order the points: probably here into lexical, connotative, & extended

4) The thesis we will use follows: A clearer understanding of faith can be achieved by reviewing lexical definitions, associated meanings and ideas, and finally looking at some examples of faithful men.

5) Using the seven sentence technique, the skeleton of the essay can now be framed.

intro:	Many passions and ideas motivate men to action.
thesis:	A clearer understanding of faith can be achieved by reviewing lexical definitions, associated meanings and ideas, and finally looking at some examples of faithful men.
1st BP:	A good place to begin when defining terms is with the dictionary since it establishes a general standard and provides a starting point.
2nd BP:	Meanings and ideas commonly associated with a term are also helpful in gaining insight into the full meaning of a term.
3rd BP:	Finally, some examples of those exhibiting faith will give a fuller idea of faith and how it is manifested.
restatement:	Having examined the dictionary, checked out various connotations, and viewed three examples of faith being exhibited, we can see more clearly what faith really is.
final:	Faith is something everyone has, and it should be examined carefully as it is the basis for one's entire life.

6-7) The body paragraphs can then be fleshed out, and the introductory and concluding paragraphs can be devised and put into place. After creating the rough draft, proof read for mechanical errors and general flow of the presentation and make the necessary changes. Remember with this essay, you have to be careful of your punctuation of words used out of context. See the next page for an example of the definition essay.

Faith as Found in Man

Many passions and ideas motivate men to action. Single ideas, however, are generally related to a series of other ideas. These ideas or ideals often come together to form some sort of overall philosophy by which a person operates his or her life. In a general way, we refer to a person's set of ideas as their faith. A clearer understanding of faith can be achieved by reviewing lexical definitions, associated meanings and ideas, and finally looking at some examples of faithful men.

A good place to begin when defining terms is with the dictionary since it establishes a general standard and provides a starting point. Some synonyms for the term *faith* are *belief*, *trust*, *loyalty*, and *religion*. Antonyms would *unbelief*, *mistrust*, and *doubt*. The term comes to us in English from the Latin word, *fidere*, which means to trust. Thus, a good working definition would be having complete trust or confidence, or having an unquestioning belief in some person or idea.

Meanings and ideas commonly associated with a term are also helpful in gaining insight into the full meaning of a term. Ideas often associated with faith are happiness, assurance, safety, comfort, and probably the idea of being right. Sometimes blind obedience comes to mind as well, but this is often in a negative sense and doesn't seem to reflect any thoughtfulness. It is apparent from looking around that faith brings some assurance and stability to life and is used by many to cope with the difficulties and circumstances of life in which they find themselves.

Finally, some examples of those exhibiting faith will give a fuller idea of faith and how it is manifested. From Scripture we can draw many examples of faithful men. Abraham left his home and offered his son as a sacrifice on faith while Noah built an ark and gathered animals in faith. Christopher Columbus set sail looking for new world across uncharted seas with the faith he would find that world. In a more modern setting, we see astronauts blasting into space with the faith that the rocket or space shuttle they are riding will bring them back. Faith causes men to do many things.

Having examined the dictionary, checked out various connotations, and viewed three examples of faith being exhibited, we can see more clearly what faith really is. According to the dictionary, faith is a belief in which a person has complete trust. We associate the ideas of confidence and assurance with the idea of faith. Both in Scripture and the world we see many examples of men who had faith to go ahead where others would not. Faith is something everyone has, and it should be examined carefully as it is the basis for one's entire life.

THE PROCESS ESSAY

The process pattern is one of the most used and useful patterns in exposition. It is normally expressed as a set of directions, a *how to* scenario of some sort. The function of the process essay is to present the reader with an orderly and systematic method of doing something.

A. There are two levels in the process pattern: 1) giving simple directions, and 2) giving information about how something is, was, or should be done. The first level is easy to write but difficult to make interesting. The second level allows for more creativity due to the greater variety of subject matter.

B. The order of the three body paragraphs follows the actual order of the steps necessary to complete the process. You must observe a chronological (time) order if your essay is to make sense to the reader.

C. All steps vital to completing the process must be included. It is also important to assume very little on the part of the reader. Give thorough instructions to ensure successful completion and understanding of the project.

D. If you are explaining how something was done in the past, it is best to provide a specific setting or instance when the process occurred as described in your essay.

E. You may wish to emphasize a time order by using transitional words such as first, next, finally, and so on. References to specific times or dates when dealing with a process from the past is also quite acceptable.

Here is a general procedure for constructing a process essay.

1) Decide upon a directional or informational level.
2) Pick a subject that lends itself to the mode chosen above.
3) List all the equipment, conditions, and steps involved.
4) Arrange the above into their proper time order.
5) Divide #3 into three logical subheads for paragraphing.
6) Determine specific thesis statement.
7) Develop details for each paragraph.
8) Set up the seven sentence skeleton.
9) Write the rough draft.

WORKING IT THROUGH

1) We decide our general approach. For this illustration, we will use the informational level and give a general scenario of how to do something.

2) Next we pick the subject. In this case it will be about selecting a used car.

3) Brainstorm for a list: test driving, second opinions, researching the market, shopping around, deciding what car is needed, setting price limits, and so forth.

4) & 5) These will occur somewhat simultaneously. As we arrange the items, we can see that it is necessary to do some homework first, then go out and see what is available, and finally test the cars that fit the criteria.

6) Our thesis will be as follows: When selecting a car for yourself, you can best profit by first gathering information, then shopping the market, and finally testing the cars.

7) Now we can line out the details per paragraph that we might use. The first body paragraph will include reading the ads, deciding what is needed, getting a copy of the Kelly Blue Book, and talking to friends about dealers and salesmen. The second body paragraph should discuss getting information about cars that are for sale, having a check list for comparison, and visually inspecting the vehicles. The third body paragraph will describe the actual test drive and getting a second opinion from a mechanic.

8) Using the seven sentence technique, the skeleton of the essay can now be framed.

intro:	You will all make a few major purchases during your lifetime.
thesis:	When selecting a car for yourself, you can best profit by first gathering information, then shopping the market, and finally testing the cars.
1st BP:	The first step in selecting any car is to gather information about what the market has to offer and how that matches up with your personal needs.
2nd BP:	The next basic step is get out and see the actual cars for sale and get specific information on them for comparison purposes.
3rd BP:	The last step prior to purchase is to test drive the vehicles under consideration and check them out more thoroughly.
restatement:	By gathering information about the market and your needs first, then carefully shopping the market, and finally doing some test drives, it is possible to obtain a good deal in the car market.
final:	Next time you decide you need a car, be sure to plan your shopping instead of just going out and being sold by some slick salesman.

9) The body paragraphs can now be fleshed out with details; the introductory and concluding paragraphs can be devised and put into place. After creating the rough draft, proof read for mechanical errors and general flow of the presentation and make the necessary changes. See the next page for an example.

Buying Right

You will all make a few major purchases during your lifetime. Most people in America look forward to buying their own home, and that's a very major purpose. Almost everyone in America, however, makes some other purchases that cost more money than the usual food and clothes. The normal need for transportation in today's world sends most of us at some time or another to the car lot. When selecting a car for yourself, you can best profit by first gathering information, then shopping the market, and...finally testing the cars.

The first step in selecting any car is to gather information about what the market has to offer and how that matches up with your personal needs. Personal needs are key here. Do you want a vehicle to haul around a family of six, or are you interested in a car for just getting one person back and forth to work. You need to ask some questions and prioritize the answers. Once you have an idea of what you need, you can look over what the market has to offer. Don't go out looking before you identify your needs.

The next basic step is get out and see the actual cars for sale and get specific information on them for comparison purposes. You need to have a price range in mind and a general idea of the type of car you want. Look through the newspapers and the other printed magazines that are available locally. Focus on what you are looking for and discard the rest. Then it's time to go looking on the lots or calling on individuals who have advertised something that caught your interest.

The last step prior to purchase is to test drive the vehicles under consideration and check them out more thoroughly. You can get some idea by driving the vehicle around yourself. It is handy to have a check list of questions with you. Does it feel comfortable; does it handle well, does it start easily; what are the tires like; is there documentation available on past servicing? There's lots of questions to ask. If you get serious about a particular car, you might ask to take it to a mechanic of your choice for an evaluation.

By gathering information about the market and your needs first, then carefully shopping the market, and finally doing some test drives, it is possible to obtain a good deal in the car market. Figuring out your needs will greatly help determine the kind of vehicle you will be interested in. Do your homework in the newspapers and other printed material before you actually go looking at cars. Before actually purchasing the car, be sure to go through a good checklist of points you want to be satisfied on. Next time you decide you need a car, be sure to plan your shopping instead of just going out and being sold by some slick salesman.

THE ANALOGY ESSAY

The function of the analogy essay is to describe or explain a complicated, difficult or unfamiliar subject by relating it to something familiar to the reader. The analogy is a picture making comparison; it can also be thought of as an extended metaphor. The analogy will always break down at some point since the two subjects are never completely alike. The point is to use the similarities to illustrate the former in terms of the latter.

A. Analogy essays illustrate by comparing three basic similarities of the subject and its related item. These three similarities are stated in the thesis statement. Generally the purpose is to clarify understanding or make some point regarding the central subject.

B. The three major categories or subdivisions should be of similar or equal value in importance and should be clearly identified.

C. The subject or item used as the comparison should be familiar to the readers, at least most of them.

D. The two subjects should have meaningful characteristics in common and should be comparable in similar terms.

Here is a general procedure for constructing an analogy essay.

1) Pick a topic to describe & the point to be made.
2) Find a suitable subject for comparison.
3) Brainstorm for similarities.
4) Arrange and categorize in order of probable use.
5) Determine a specific thesis statement.
6) Develop suitable subdivisions and details for each main category.
7) Set up the seven sentence skeleton.
8) Write the rough draft.

WORKING IT THROUGH

1) We decide our general topic area. For this illustration, we will talk about the stock market. Our point will be that it is easy to learn how it works.

2) Next we find a suitable subject for comparison. In this case we will use a flea market.

3) Brainstorming for similarities we find the following: both are places to buy and sell, commissions are charged for every transaction, the law of supply and demand affects the prices, limited goods are available, multiple sources for trading exist, prices fluctuate constantly, some trading goes on all the time the market is open.

4) Three categories emerge: the people involved, the goods traded, and the forces of the market place. The order seems to fit a *who, what, why* scenario.

5) Our working thesis will be as follows: It is easy to learn the basics of the stock market by viewing it as a flea market and looking at the traders, the goods, and the market forces at work.

6) This step is closely related to the two previous steps and is performed somewhat simultaneously. For the first category we could compare brokerage houses and salesmen with tables and individuals. Commissions and profits as well as a central clearing house could also be mentioned. The goods reflect the stocks; there is a wide variety of quality, choice, price, and potential. Market forces are reflected in supply, demand, price, and current market trends.

7) Using the seven sentence technique, the skeleton of the essay can now be framed.

intro:	Everyone is interested in making money.
thesis:	It is easy to learn the basics of the stock market by viewing it as a flea market and looking at the traders, the goods, and the market forces at work.
1st BP:	First we will note that all trades are handled by some middleman, a trader or broker of some sort.
2nd BP:	Our second focus is that the goods in a flea market are somewhat representative of the stocks in the stock market.
3rd BP:	Finally, we will see that the market forces in a flea market reflect to a large extent the same forces found in the stock market.
restatement:	Having seen how the flea market operates with its traders, goods, and market forces, we should now know the basics of what goes on in the stock market as well.
final:	Now you should have no fear of investing in the stock market since it is really quite similar in many respects to the weekend flea markets that you already may know and enjoy.

8) The body paragraphs can now be fleshed out with details; the introductory and concluding paragraphs can be devised and put into place. After creating the rough draft, proof read for mechanical errors and general flow of the presentation and make the necessary changes. See the next page for an example.

A Tale of Two Markets

Everyone is interested in making money. Money can be made by working, investing, lending at interest, and by buying and selling, also called trading. People buy and sell all kinds of things: real estate, new and used goods, commodities, and stocks just to name a few. More and more people are becoming interested in the stock market. It is easy to learn the basics of the stock market by viewing it as a flea market and looking at the traders, the goods, and the market forces at work.

First we will note that all trades are handled by some middleman, a trader or broker of some sort. In a flea market, there are lots of different folks sitting around behind tables and such. Those people are the traders. They have a variety of goods to sell. Some of them sell on consignment, meaning they don't own the goods but are willing to sell them for a commission. These folks are somewhat analogous to the stock broker who does the paperwork for a stock trade. He proffers the stocks and takes a small commission just as the fellow at the table sells a knickknack and takes a piece of the selling price for himself.

Our second focus is that the goods in a flea market are somewhat representative of the stocks in the stock market. At flea markets you can find all kinds of things. Some of the stuff is junk. Some of the items might be real treasures at low prices. The prices vary and to some degree will be adjusted to what the buyer and seller can agree upon. The same is true of the stock market. Some stocks are grossly overpriced while others of good value are way under priced for some reason. Good deals and bad deals are to found in both the flea market and the stock market.

Finally, we will see that the market forces in a flea market reflect to a large extent the same forces found in the stock market. Market forces are what we might call supply and demand. In a flea market you might find a one of a kind item. The stock market is not that way. Both markets offer plenty of variety; you can buy stocks or goods of all kinds, some cheap and some expensive. Trends are also prevalent. In the stock market you will find fads where many people seem to want one kind of stock but ignore others. The same holds true at flea markets; at times people are focusing on dolls or trains or teacups or whatever. People's passions for things run hot and cold.

Having seen how the flea market operates with its traders, goods, and market forces, we should now know the basics of what goes on in the stock market as well. In both markets something is bought and sold for a commission or a profit. Whether it is stocks or flea market goods, the deals can be good or bad depending on the item and its price. Common forces are also found; supply, demand, price, and even fads affect both markets. Now you should have no fear of investing in the stock market since it is really quite similar in many respects to the weekend flea markets that you may already know and enjoy.

THE CAUSE & EFFECT ESSAY

The cause and effect pattern is useful when analyzing an event or attempting to get to the bottom of some action. The function of the cause and effect essay is to give reasons as to why something has happened or perhaps will happen in the future.

A. The three body paragraphs each deal with a particular cause or reason which is a part of the overall argument.

B. The order of the three body paragraphs usually follows the actual order of occurrence of the three causes. This may be altered if no particular time frame is evident; then an order of importance is used with the least important first and the most important last.

C. Causes fall into two types, immediate and ultimate. The search for ultimate causes is generally beyond the scope of a short essay. It is best to stick with the immediate causes. An example should suffice: effect = an auto accident, immediate cause = speeding, ultimate cause = predestined. Note that not only prior events and actions are to be examined, attitudes and motivations are also taken into consideration.

D. Avoid fallacious reasoning when searching for causes. Just because one event precedes another, it does not always follow that A causes B. For instance, the letter A precedes B in the alphabet but does not cause B to exist.

E. It is necessary to show an adequate connection between a statement of cause and the effect. To do so it may be necessary to quote recognized authorities, supply statistics, give examples, or offer some other information to clarify the connection.

Here is a general procedure for constructing a cause and effect essay.

1) Pick a subject and set it up as a question, why/how....
2) Answer your question with reasons/causes.
3) Subdivide your reasons into three basic categories.
4) Arrange the three categories/causes into a logical order.
5) Determine specific thesis statement.
6) Develop details for each paragraph.
7) Set up the seven sentence skeleton.
8) Write the rough draft.

WORKING IT THROUGH

1) We decide our general topic area. For this illustration, we will talk about the Jim Jones mass suicide in Guyana. Our topic set in question form follows: Why did this mass suicide occur?

2) Next we list various reasons: false religious belief, programmed minds, follow the leader mentalities, fear, hysteria, force, and catalyst murders.

3) Three probable subdivisions might be particular religious practices, specific conditions at the time, and the immediate prior events.

4) The arrangement of the three divisions above will suffice.

5) Our thesis will be as follows: A close look at the specific religious practices, the particular conditions at the actual event, and the immediate prior events should yield an understanding of why the mass suicide of Jim Jones and his followers took place.

6) Now we can line out the details per paragraph that we might use. The first body paragraph can include their view of the afterlife, the teaching that suicide would lead from persecution to the promised land, and their herd mentality. The second body paragraph will deal with the fears they had, the hysteria and emotion of the situation and the force used to make everyone comply. The third body paragraph will describe the killings of the congressman and newsmen a few hours before and how it affected the leaders and the group.

7) Using the seven sentence technique, the skeleton of the essay can now be framed.

intro:	When a number of people die in an incident, we often call it a tragedy.
thesis:	A close look at the specific religious practices, the particular conditions at the actual event, and the immediate prior events should yield an understanding of why the mass suicide of Jim Jones and his followers took place.
1st BP:	Certain peculiar teachings of Jim Jones set up his followers to see suicide as a viable alternative to life.
2nd BP:	The emotional climate of leaders and followers at the time can best be described as highly charged and even desperate.
3rd BP:	The killings which took place directly before the mass suicide probably created the need for some atoning or escapist action.
restatement:	Due to the mind set caused by the teaching, the strain of situation, and the prior killings that took place, it is somewhat understandable why the mass suicide of Jim Jones and his followers happened.
final:	Beware of false prophets and phony religions; they might just cost you your life.

8) The body paragraphs can now be fleshed out with details; the introductory and concluding paragraphs can be devised and put into place. After creating the rough draft, proof read for mechanical errors and general flow of the presentation and make the necessary changes. See the example on the next page.

71

A Look at the Jim Jones Tragedy

When a number of people die in an incident, we often call it a tragedy. Tragedies take different forms. Some are natural events such as earthquakes or hurricanes while others involve some accident such as a boat sinking or a train derailing. Sometimes, however, tragedies are definitely caused by man and his actions. False religions often have a way of destroying their followers in bizarre manners. A close look at the specific religious practices, the particular conditions at the actual event, and the immediate prior events should yield an understanding of why the mass suicide of Jim Jones and his followers took place.

Certain peculiar teachings of Jim Jones set up his followers to see suicide as a viable alternative to life. Jones taught a peculiar view of the afterlife, so dying and moving beyond this plane of existence was something desirable, something to look forward to. This life was looked at as a life of persecution while the next life was one of promise and hope. Suicide was taught as a viable way to transition to the next life. There was also a strong herd mentality in this group; they were taught to think and act alike and to follow their leaders in all things. The evidence for this was the group had removed themselves from the United States and gone to Guyana to escape persecution.

The emotional climate of leaders and followers at the time can best be described as highly charged and even desperate. The fact they all felt persecuted in this world weighed upon them. Since parents and relatives had called for an investigation, the group felt even more pressure. Surely the world was out to get them. Life in this world was fast becoming a nightmare. Their fleeing the United States had solved nothing. The only escape left was to flee the world.

The killings which took place directly before the mass suicide probably created the need for some atoning or escapist action. A congressman who had come to investigate and his aide were killed by some of the members. Obviously now the group was under condemnation of the law. What could they do to atone for the killings, and what could they do to escape their rapidly decaying situation. Evidence after the fact shows that some force was used on members to drink the poisoned lemonade. This group self-destructed en masse.

Due to the mind set caused by the teaching, the strain of situation, and the prior killings that took place, it is somewhat understandable why the mass suicide of Jim Jones and his followers happened. Escaping this persecuting world the paradise of the next world was one of their primary beliefs. The leaders were emotionally agitated and unstable due to the immediate circumstances. The final blow of killing the congressman and his aide probably forced them to take some definitive action which ended in mass suicide. Beware of false prophets and phony religions; they might just cost you your life.

THE COMPARISON ESSAY

Often it is useful to organize a five paragraph essay around a comparison of two similar ideas or items. Each body paragraph focuses on a subset or area of the comparison. The function of the comparison essay is to show two ideas or items in relation to one another, often to show the superiority of one over the other.

A. Comparison essays list three major areas of the subjects compared in the thesis statement. Generally the purpose is to show likenesses and differences in such a way as to promote one subject over the other.

B. The typical information found in each body paragraph will be details about the area of comparison chosen. Some logical order of presentation should be evident.

C. The comparisons should follow an order; generally the least important areas are considered first with the more important areas coming last. This order should be apparent both within a given paragraph and among the paragraphs themselves. Putting the strongest or most favorable comparison last makes the strongest impression on the reader.

D. Obviously the comparison essay not only compares but also contrasts the ideas or subjects. The differences and likenesses are woven together to make a full picture. All comparisons simply show the degree of compatibility between the two subjects; at some point the difference outweighs the similarity.

E. Whenever possible in this type of essay, the qualities of one subject should be expressed in terms of the compared subject. This is easiest when there are measurable attributes of some sort; for instance, the popularity of product X is three times that of product Y.

Here is a general procedure for constructing a comparison essay.

1) Determine the two subjects for comparison.
2) Brainstorm; list all categories that might be compared.
3) Subdivide those categories into three natural divisions.
4) Decide which subject is most favorable.
5) Arrange the divisions from least to greatest importance.
6) Write the thesis statement.
7) Arrange the details of each body paragraph from least to greatest.
8) Set up the seven sentence skeleton.
9) Write the rough draft.

WORKING IT THROUGH

1) We decide our topic is to compare home school with public school.

2) Now we brainstorm for the possible areas of comparison: subject variety, class size, outside influences and pressures, amount of individual instruction, overall philosophy, flexibility in schedule, social interaction, standards, physical plant, quality of instruction, dead time (commuting, lunch hours, assemblies, etc.)

3) The next job is to place the above items into three natural categories. For purposes here we will use academics, philosophies, and associated conditions.

4) Home school is the most favorable subject.

5) The categories in order of importance should be associated conditions, academics, and philosophies.

6) The thesis: A comparison of associated conditions, academic performance, and philosophical direction of home school and public school will provide information for making an intelligent choice between the two alternatives.

7) We arrange the first body paragraph details in a possible order of least to greatest importance. Note the favoring of home school by placing the most positive comparisons last with the least positive first. The other two body paragraphs would be similarly arranged.

    1. physical plant comparison - gyms, stages, libraries, etc.
    2. physical danger to student on campus
    3. dead/wasted time
    4. flexibility & opportunity to meet specific student needs

8) Using the seven sentence technique, the skeleton of the essay can now be framed.

intro:	Choice is a common cry in political circles today and is fast becoming an issue in many areas of life.
thesis:	A comparison of associated conditions, academic performance, and philosophical direction of home school and public school will provide information for making an intelligent choice between the two alternatives.
1st BP:	A brief look at some of the associated conditions of both types of schools will be helpful at this point.
2nd BP:	Academic performance and opportunity is a second area of comparison that deserves strong attention.
3rd BP:	Probably the most important area of comparison is the philosophical direction of each school type and the various outworking of those directions.
restatement:	After looking at the respective conditions, academics and philosophies of home and public schools, it is apparent that the home school offers significant advantages over the public system.
final:	May the choice imposed on children be for their best benefit and betterment, both now and in the future.

9) The body paragraphs can now be fleshed out with details; the introductory and concluding paragraphs can be devised and put into place. After creating the rough draft, be sure to proof read for mechanical errors and general flow of presentation. Make the necessary changes for your final draft.

Educational Choices

Choice is a common cry in political circles today and is fast becoming an issue in many areas of life. People are very jealous of their rights to choose on issues, and education is an example. Various formats for education exist in the United States today. We generally divide the options into public and non-public education. Among the non-public schools we find private schools, Christian schools and home schools. Let's compare the two most unlike systems, public schools and home schools. A comparison of associated conditions, academic performance, and philosophical direction of home school and public school will provide information for making an intelligent choice between the two alternatives.

A brief look at some of the associated conditions of both types of schools will be helpful at this point. Public schools have facilities that often include gyms, stages, libraries, band rooms, science labs and the like. Home schools rarely have any of the above. On the other hand, there are problems created by having a number of students together which are not encountered in a home school. Certainly no one will deny the possibility of physical danger is higher in public situation that it probably is in the home. Just moving large numbers of people around from class to class and to and from school creates a lot of unproductive time that is not replicated in a home school situation. While the public school often has many options for classes and specialists in some areas, the flexibility of the home school to meet specific individual needs is unmatched in many ways.

Academic performance and opportunity is a second area of comparison that deserves strong attention. The public schools, particularly at the upper levels, often have teachers who are able to offer expertise in particular areas such as math or science or agriculture. On the other hand, the home school teacher normally doesn't even possess a teaching degree. However, the proof is not in what is available but what is learned. Here the home schooled person excels. On the various standardized tests, home schoolers as a group always test better than their public school counterparts as a group. Thus, we can say that at least on the tests, the home schoolers are better prepared academically than their peers in the public school.

Probably the most important area of comparison is the philosophical direction of each school type and the various outworking of those directions. The public school claims neutrality in this area. That is false. The public school has a general bias, and the individual teachers also have their own slants on things. Looking at the trends in the public system of education in the United States as evidenced today, anyone can see the direction to multiculturalism and permissiveness. Home schoolers are not united in their philosophies, but each home school teacher can pick what he or she thinks is best for his or her children. This is very positive for the student since the same values that are taught in the home school are generally modeled by the parents; thus, there is no confusion in the student's mind regarding conflicting systems.

After looking at the respective conditions, academics and philosophies of home and public schools, it is apparent that the home school offers significant advantages over the public system. Positive options are not necessarily related to large numbers of students. Academically, home schoolers just do better as a group than those in public school. Most importantly, the home schooled student is taught a value system consistent with what his or her parents believe. May the choice imposed on children be for their best benefit and betterment, both now and in the future.

SECTION 3

Practical Applications

BOOK REPORTS

In this section you will find some practical application of the five paragraph essay. In particular, you will find out some methods of how to prepare a decent book report. The book report probably generates some mixed emotions. Writing the reports is definitely not as much fun as reading the books; at least for me it never was. However, as a teacher, I can honestly say that reading the reports wasn't that much fun either. Yet everyone more or less agrees that book reports must have some value; after all, they continue to be assigned generation after generation. Let's take a look the following: the purposes of book reports and some examples of outlines that can be assigned as is or modified. You will find three different examples/formats.

It seems that the basic purpose of a book report is to provide some feedback on how you, the student, related to the book that was assigned. In some cases it may be that the report is tacked on to the reading so as to ensure that you actually read the book. Of course, if you are creative, you can produce a report without reading the book if the reporting format is not designed well. If a specific book is assigned, a very specific series of answers can be requested in the report, but this means that the teacher must read the book or have some working knowledge of what the book contains. It also means everyone in the class would probably read that same book, but in that case you would probably just have a test on it. If any book in a given genre is acceptable, the teacher must then have a different set of questions on hand. These questions must be applicable to a variety of books instead of just one particular book.

The more information your teacher gives you, the easier it should be to write the report. Sometimes, however, you might just be assigned a book report with little else to go on. That's where the formats you will see in this book could be of great help.

Books can be classed in groups. Non-fiction books are generally handled differently from fiction books although there is a blurring between fictional biographies and histories as opposed to their counterparts on the non-fiction side. The type of book and the teacher's motivations for assigning the reading must be taken into account before questions on a report can be properly constructed and answered. Let's focus primarily on works of fiction since that is what you will most often be asked to read. Following this general explanation, you will find three book report forms. They are for your information. Put them to use. Perhaps your teacher might have you utilize one or more of them.

Historical fiction books are good to assign for a variety of reasons. They give a flavor of the times; they may include some real historical figures. The stories usually have elements of adventure and action that makes them more palatable to readers than the normally dry history of textbooks. Certain cultural patterns and customs from the period are woven into the story through the setting, the speech, and the various events that take place. Historical fiction is a good way to become acquainted with a given period of time and a particular culture and geographic area, and it is generally somewhat enjoyable to read.

What questions might you be asked regarding an historical novel? Certainly you should be able to identify the time and place in which the book occurs. The setting of a novel precludes certain behaviors on the parts of the characters. A reader develops a limited set of expectations from the setting. A knight in shining armor is not expected to act in the same way as a cowboy or a pirate. Settings need to be identified, even in a general way such as Middle Ages in Europe. After identifying the setting, you might then be asked for three or four ideas or customs that are associated with the setting. If you aren't asked, you can supply them and make an impression on your teacher.

All stories have plots. The plot revolves around some problem that needs to be resolved. This is where most students want to retell the story. Don't do it! Limit your response to a paragraph or perhaps five to seven sentences. The idea is to reduce the story to its bare essence. A prince tries to regain the throne his evil uncle has usurped. A major rancher is stripped of his power because he gets too greedy. The young pirate must make a decision about right and wrong and how he works this through. Reducing the story to the basic problem and how it is solved in just a few sentences is not easy, but a reasonable job can be accomplished with some thought.

In almost every story there is some central character the story revolves around. Often this person is called the hero or heroine. Rarely is a villain the central character. You should be able to describe the hero both physically and spiritually. You might be asked for a physical description and some particulars regarding the hero's personality. Other information might include how the central character relates and treats others in the book. Was the person believable; could you identify with the hero or heroine? What did you like and dislike about the central character? Were there any instances in which you would have acted differently from the central character? Why? How might that have changed the story?

As you read, you should be gathering information and impressions. One favorite question of mine was always to ask for three items of historical interest that the reader learned from the book. Answers in the past have varied from the trivial to the profound. One student mentions that heating a stone castle with fireplaces took lots of wood; another comments that the nobility had all the horses while a third says that the large crossbow could shoot clear through an armored man at 100 yards. All the answers are valid since they represent some idea gleaned from the book. Closely tied to historical facts are the impressions you have gained. These should be more wide ranging and need to be supported by details from the story. A sample answer might be that poor people had it very rough; they had only huts to live in, had a poor diet of roots, and were made to go to war with only their wooden rakes and forks.

Another popular form of book often assigned is the biography. This book is about a person's life or a portion of it. Biographies are very similar to historical fiction except they deal with a real person in a real setting. Below you will get a look at a typical biography book report.

Every book report needs to mention certain statistical information. This is usually covered very near the beginning. It mentions the author's name, the title of the book, the publisher, when the book was written, how many pages it contains, and perhaps even where the book could be obtained and for how much.

The report is to consist of five paragraphs. The general content of each paragraph is listed. In some cases particular sentences are to contain specific information. Let's do a quick run through of the various paragraphs in a biographical book.

The first sentence of the first paragraph needs to grab attention. After that the statistical information mentioned above can be worked in. Then a thesis statement needs to be made. The three body paragraphs will talk about biographical material, the theme of the book, and how it applies to the reader. The final paragraph sums up your position as the reader where likes and dislikes are mentioned as well as recommendations pro and con.

Further information about each of the paragraphs is given on the assignment sheet. The structure of a five paragraph essay is quite adaptable for this report, but it could be overlaid on almost any other book report as well. It is simply one example of an external format in which to place the information. For the more creative, a biography report could be written in question and answer form as some kind of interview where you would ask the character questions and make up responses. Hopefully your teacher will tell you what information and opinions will be required as far as content in the report. This is essential so that you will know what information to look for while reading the book. Again, if no guidelines are given, then knowing at least one format for this kind of report will be helpful in constructing your report.

Biographies are a rich source of material. Many good ones have been written about great men and women reflecting positive ideals that should be passed on to each generation. Missionaries, martyrs, scientists, statesmen, preachers, explorers, pioneers, all kinds of people have been written about, and the stories about them are interesting because they are real people with real problems.

General fiction books have totally imaginative characters. There will always be some setting in which the story takes place, but it may be anything from a real time and place to the utterly fantastic. Much of modern fantasy and science fiction has settings of this sort. Just because the setting is totally imaginary does not mean that a book is of no value. Ideas can be brought up and discussed seriously in such books. For instance, one science fiction story deals with a future time when body part transplants are common operations. Because of this, a market and trade for such parts comes into being. Some people are victimized by others for parts of their bodies. The whole moral issue of individual value is raised. Is it right for one person of esteem to require the body part of someone considered expendable?

One curious fact is that no matter what the setting of most books written today, the people in the book think and act like contemporary Americans. There is no getting around it. If they were really different, we couldn't relate to the characters and probably would find the book dissatisfactory.

When reading general fiction, you are often given quite a bit of leeway as to what is said in your report. Generally the report is a justification for your perspective on the book: was it worth reading or not? Again, you are provided with a five paragraph essay structure. Of course, it could be changed to a question and answer situation, an oral presentation, or whatever other format might be decided upon. Note that the information is broken up into three basic areas plus the statistical matter. Plot, characters, and style are the three used here; however, style might be replaced with a discussion of the central theme and the validity of its conclusion or even its presentation. One idea that is always good to include is whether or not the central idea of the book squares with Scripture. What Biblical principles are sustained or violated in the book? You should think on these questions as you read.

When reading fiction I suggest you take a few notes. Here's how to do it, especially if you have to read the book in pieces over time. First, make a single sentence summary of each chapter. You should identify the single most important event in the chapter. This will help you review and understand the plot. Second, write down the name of each new character and describe that person with 5-8 separate words. You might say things such as loving, overweight, stressed out, handsome, and so forth. You should also note the relationships they have with others; they are lovers, enemies, husbands, parents, etc. of other characters in the book. You should also note the setting; write down place names & pertinent descriptors and note the basic time frame. Give the year, season and date if applicable.

Aside from the statistical information, most of what you write will be your impression. Your opinions should be justified from details taken from the book, however. Further, some opinions ought to also be measured against God's Word, especially those that deal with moral issues.

Immediately following you will find three outlines and suggestions for book reports on historical fiction, a biography, and general fiction. Study them over; perhaps your teacher might assign one or more of them to you. If not, produce a book report for some other class using the guidelines given.

HISTORICAL FICTION BOOK REPORT GUIDE

What follows are basic questions you will want to answer about any historical fiction book. Once you have the answers, you can craft a five paragraph essay around the information. You don't have to use all the information, but it helps to have it available. If your teacher asks particular questions, you will certainly want to answer those as well.

1. Get the statistical information on the book.

  a) title of book
  b) author
  c) publication/copyright date
  d) publisher
  e) # of pages

2. Give the setting: time
                          place

3. Identify the basic conflict or problem in the story.

4. Explain briefly how the conflict/problem is resolved.

5. The HERO: give the central character's name:
       describe the him/her physically:
       mention three outstanding personality characteristics:

6. List three items of historical interest you learned from the book.

7. Give three of your impressions of the era covered by the book, and supply details to support your arguments.

8. Mention anything else you want to about the book.

9. Was the author pushing a particular viewpoint or position? If so, what?

From the above, you should be able to craft a good thesis statement, probably a value judgment about the book. Is it worth reading or not? Body paragraph subjects might be interesting historical facts, plot, characters, impressions of the times, themes in history, or even author bias.

FIVE PARAGRAPH BOOK REPORT - BIOGRAPHY

Here's an outline for a biography book report. It is structured around a five paragraph format. I'll use S1 for sentence one and so forth.

INTRODUCTORY PARAGRAPH

S1 general interest catcher
S2+ - name of book, author, publisher, copyright, type of book, # of pages
NOTE: instead of a typical introductory paragraph, you can create one that includes the statistical information.
S(last) - thesis statement: includes 1) purpose, & 2) outline overview

Here's an example of an introductory paragraph built along the lines given above.

Some of the finest adventure is written in the form of biography. *Shackleton's Boat Journey* is one such adventure. It was written by F.A. Worsley and is primarily about Sir Ernest Shackleton and his trip to Antarctica. The version I read was written in 1977 and published by W. W. Norton & Company as a Jove paperback book of 190 pages. Looking at the biographical material, the theme of the book, and the personal applications in this book, we can determine if it is a good book to read.

BODY PARAGRAPH #1

S1 topic sentence (biographical material)
S2+ setting, main characters, life summary

BODY PARAGRAPH #2

S1 topic sentence (idea/theme of book)
S2+ main point of book, author's bias, Biblical principles upheld/denied, justifications

BODY PARAGRAPH #3

S1 topic sentence (personal applications)
S2+ knowledge gained, uses in personal life

CONCLUDING PARAGRAPH

S1 restatement of thesis
S2 summary statement of body paragraph #1
S3 summary statement of body paragraph #2
S4 summary statement of body paragraph #3
S5 an appeal to read or avoid the book

Somewhere in those three body paragraphs you should comment on the strengths and weaknesses as you see them in the appropriate paragraphs. For instance, if you thought the main character was unbelievable, you would mention that in the first paragraph, assuming that's where you put the biographical material. Depending on your ultimate recommendation, you would need to order the three body paragraphs from weakest to strongest to help make your point.

FICTION BOOK REPORT GUIDE

1. Each of the paragraphs should be about equal in length. Be especially careful of paragraph two; do not retell the whole story.
2. Be sure to have a thesis statement properly placed at the end of the introductory paragraph.
3. Be sure to use examples to backup your statements.

INTRODUCTORY PARAGRAPH

attention getter of some sort
title of the book, author, publication/copyright date, and publisher
general genre it fits (mystery, romance, etc.)
thesis to include: plot, characterization, and author's style (the basis why you like/dislike the book)

BODY PARAGRAPH #1

plot summary - includes the following: setting, basic conflict, and its resolution

BODY PARAGRAPH #2

characterization - discuss 3 characters
   protagonist (hero)   antagonist (villain)   any other character of your choice
for each one mention the following:
   strong and weak points   credibility (are they real, life-like?)
   identifiability (could you relate to them, be in their shoes?)

BODY PARAGRAPH #3

style - how does the author handle the following:
   use of detail (appropriate, accurate)
   use of dialogue and description
   flow of the story (dull spots, continuous action, logical?)
   ease of reading (vocabulary, dialect, intricate plot?)
   prominence of theme, makes the point clear

CONCLUDING PARAGRAPH

general summary
   restatement of thesis
   summation of each body paragraph in order
   final recommendation to others regarding the book

Remember, the order of the three body paragraphs would be dependent on what you thought was the weakest to the strongest arguments for your position as reflected in your recommendation. If you thought the plot was the worst facet of the book and you were telling people to avoid the book, then you would put the body paragraph about plot last. If you were trying to make a case to read the book and still thought the plot was the weakest point in the book, you would put that paragraph first in the body.

TEST QUESTIONS

The farther along you get in school, the more likely it is you will run into the essay question. Practically speaking, on some essays you can get by with a good paragraph. Other times you will need to produce something of greater length. Here is where having the five paragraph formats will suit you well.

First we have to presuppose that you know enough to answer the question. All the organization in the world won't help you if you haven't got the correct information to fill in your answer. But let's assume you do have the information. What do you do then? Here's a series of steps you can and should take.

1. Jot down a number of specifics as notes to yourself. These would be specific facts or ideas that are pertinent to answering the question. Write them down where you can reference them while writing.
2. Sort the information into categories or subtopics. This will help you for the next step.
3. Come up with a thesis statement.
4. Figure out which of the seven formats the information naturally falls into.
5. If you have time, a seven sentence outline would help.
6. Write the essay.

Most often essays questions will be somewhat general. They will ask you discuss a subject in some fashion. The teacher is looking for a general understanding of the subject. The key is for you to be able to articulate the general ideas and back them up with certain specifics.

Here's a sampling of possible essay questions taken from various disciplines.

> Discuss the causes of the War Between the States.
> Identify the basic elements of the cubist school of art.
> Explain the digestive system in man.
> Compare and contrast Shakespeare and Marlowe as dramatists.
> Trace the progress of WWII in Europe after the US intervened.
> Explain the scientific method and give an example.
> Discuss the theory of aerobic exercise.

You get the idea. Sometimes the question will have more to it. Perhaps the Shakespeare/Marlowe question might ask for a focus on two particular plays or some facet of characterization. One question I will never forget came on a history final in college. The class was called The Roman Empire, and we spent one semester learning about it. The professor told us we would have one question on our final, and he told us the first day of the class what that question was: Discuss the rise and fall of the Roman Empire. Remember that we studied this information for 18 weeks and had to compress what we knew about it into an essay that we had to write in a three hour period.

The major difference in preparing a regular essay and writing one to answer a test question is that most of the time you don't know the test question beforehand. Thus, your time frame is a more cramped than when preparing a regular essay. Nevertheless, using the steps outlined above, you should be able to produce a credible essay under pressure. Of course, if you have a take home essay test, you will have more time to organize and gather information. In those cases, you may be expected to write a longer piece and include documentation of some sort as well.

Let's go through the process once just for drill. You will note the similarities to preparing a regular essay. The question we will answer is this: Discuss the development of the genre of novels we identify as westerns.

WORKING IT THROUGH

1. We need to put down some notes. Obviously since this is a development question, we can readily assume a historical process or at least some historical organization.

    early works   penny dreadfuls, much exaggeration, not too historically accurate
                                    flat characterization, concentration on action, Ned Buntline
    classics works   Zane Grey, fairly good history, some character development
                                      lots of description, much use of regionalisms
    modern works   Louis L'Amour, generally accurate history and geography,
                                    stylized characters, lots of action but good descriptions as well

2. The material is already in categories selected by stages of the development.
    early, classic, and modern

3. Now we need a thesis. The outline section is already a natural. We need a purpose. Since we are to answer the question, and the question wants us to discuss the development of the genre, let's say the western novel has become more stylized over time. It is important to note that your purpose should somehow reflect the question. Don't just put down lots of information. You do need to answer the question.

    Through a general tracing of the early, classical, and modern westerns, we can see how this form has developed.

4. It seems this naturally falls into the example format. Thus, we can use the three subtopics or categories of early, classical and modern and fill each subtopic with an example of an author, how characterization was done, the focus on action, and the accuracy of the geography and history. Getting a good order of the details would be helpful. Since we are trying to show the stylization of the genre, character and historical accuracy should come at the latter part of each body paragraph.

5. We've got the thesis, so the seven sentences could be quickly developed. On each test it would be your judgment call based on the time frame you have to create the answer and get it turned in.

intro:	All forms of literature develop and move through stages over time.
thesis:	Through a general tracing of the early, classical, and modern westerns, we can see how this form has developed.
BP#1	Early westerns were often called penny dreadfuls.
BP#2	The next stage in the westerns was what I will call the classical stage.
BP#3	Today's westerns represent the modern era of the genre.
restatement:	The western novel has changed over the years as we have seen by looking at the three eras of the genre.
final:	Today's western novel appears to have become stylized at this point in time.

6. From this point, the essay could be easily written by simply filling in the blanks so to speak. Mentioning a representative author of each time, the focus of the books, the historical and geographical accuracy, and the type of characters that emerge over time would constitute the basic sentences in each body paragraph.

Perhaps your teacher will do as one of my high school teachers did. Each Friday for one semester, we walked into first period to find three questions on the board, one of which we had to pick and write a five paragraph essay on. It was due in ink or typed by noon that day. Those assignments had their effect on pushing me to be a decent writer on command.

SECTION 4

Business Writing

BUSINESS LETTERS

Even with the advent of the internet and e-mail, business letters still must be written. In this section you will learn the basic formats and get some tips on how to construct a good business letter.

Three formats exist; they are called the block, modified block, and semi-block formats. This book will use the block format only since it is the easiest and the most widely used. In the block format, all information it typed flush left with one-inch margins all around the letter. That means one inch on the top, bottom, and sides. Do not indent the beginnings of paragraphs or any other portion of the letter.

Many types of business letters exist. You will find letters of application, letters of apology, letters requesting credit, letters of rejection or acceptance, and so forth. These letters have those names based on the content and purpose of the letter. All such letters have some common elements. Let's start with those. I'll identify the elements and then give you a sample.

The first item is the heading; some call it the sender's address. If you are using stationary with a letterhead, the letterhead serves as the heading. The heading consists of the name of the business and the address. If you are writing to a business and are representing yourself as a person with no business identity, put your name and your address. People differ on this. Some think your name at the bottom of the letter is sufficient.

The next item is the date. If you have a letterhead, this is the first item you would type. The date is always written out in a month-day-year fashion: January 30, 2002. Again, some people differ on this and think the date should be above the heading. Most folks think it should follow the heading. You should have one blank line between the heading and the date.

The third element is the inside address; this is the address of the recipient. You should have four blank lines between the date and the inside address. It is always best to write to a specific individual at the business to which you are writing, so try to get a name if possible. If the person has a title, be sure to use it.

Skip one line to the salutation. Use the same name found in the inside address, including their title if any. The salutation in a business letter always ends in a colon. Dear Mr. Adam Businessman:

Skip one more line to the body of the letter. Single space and left justify each paragraph within the body of the letter. Skip one line between paragraphs. The body is the text of your letter. It should clear and to the point. In business, time means money, so people don't want to waste time trying to figure out the purpose of your letter; they just want to know your concern and deal with it. Often a typical business letter consists of three short paragraphs. The first paragraph usually has a friendly introductory statement and then a statement making the point of your letter. The second paragraph justifies your point with supporting details and perhaps some background information. The final paragraph should restate your purpose and, in some cases, request an action of some kind.

Skip one line after the final paragraph; here you will have the complimentary close. Capitalize the first word of the close but no others unless required by other conventions. The close always ends with a comma. Here's some examples: Thank you, Sincerely, For Christ's church, and so forth.

Skip another four lines and type your name as you will sign it. If you are typing the letter for someone else, type the signature as they would sign it. If the signer has a title, it should follow on the next line.

If you have enclosed any other documents along with the letter, skip a line after the typed name and type Enclosure. You may list the name of the document you are including. If you have more than one document, it is a good idea to list them all by name.

BUSINESS LETTER WRITING TIPS

What follows is a number of tips for writing a good business letter.

1. Decide the specific purpose of your letter. You might list some things you want to say and then look them over. Delete any items that do not support your particular purpose.

2. Be brief. More is not better in a business letter. Make your letter plain and to the point. You might profit here by looking at the principle of condensation in the next section.

3. Make your point early. Begin with a friendly opening, but make the purpose of your letter plain in the second sentence. You might use a couple of sentences to do this, but don't go into detail. Just state your purpose and state it plainly.

4. Write naturally and honestly. Avoid stilted phrases such as "in accordance with your request" and other such verbiage. The style should be formal but not stilted. Short paragraphs are best. Be human; you are one person writing to another. If you know the reader's name, it is wise to work it into the body of the letter naturally.

5. Use the active voice; avoid passive constructions. You should know what I'm talking about. If not, ask your teacher.

6. Be pleasant. Try to put negatives in a positive way. Don't write in anger. Try to be upbeat. People respond much better to positives than negatives. This is especially true in a letter of complaint. The old say, "You can catch more flies with honey than with vinegar," comes to mind.

7. End with an action step. The end of the letter should generally suggest some action on the part of the reader. At times you might indicate you will be contacting them directly, but then be sure to do it.

8. Be professional. The letter needs to have a nice presentation. It should be on clean paper, proofed for errors, have a nice, logical format, and be easy to read. A page crowded with designs or lots of other typing distracts from your message. Pay particular attention to the capitalization and punctuation of the heading, inside address, salutation, and close.

9. If the body of the letter carries on to a second page, the name of the person you are writing to should be placed at the top left hand margin. Most letters should be kept to one page.

10. One final tip: read the letter as if it came to you. How would you react? Remember, the letter is all you have to represent you, so make a good impression with it, and don't say things you might regret later.

On the next two pages, you will find two different letters. Both are letters for information. Study them as examples and note the variations. At the bottom of the second letter is an assignment.

May 3, 2001

Mr. Adam Stark
Sales Manager
Proximity Properties
1838 NE Franklin Street
Coos Bay, OR 97420

Dear Mr. Stark:

Thank you for your latest brochure regarding the new planned development near the golf course. I am writing for more information, particularly about what is planned for the west side of the highway.

Your brochure shows homes and a recreational center adjoining the golf course, but the information on the commercial buildings to the west was vague. Mr. Stark, will this be a large shopping center, a mall, or a couple of strip malls? The information was unclear on this in the brochure. Also, there was no time frame for the commercial buildings. Can you supply such for me?

As you might suspect, I have some interest in the commercial aspect of the development and would like some more information. Please respond either by letter or fax to number given above. I'd prefer the fax.

Sincerely,

Harold Carson

. Harold Carson
Director of Development

HC:je

Notes on the above: A letterhead is used. The date follows with the inside address, a salutation, and the body of the letter. The letter is short; it asks for information and explains how the information should be delivered. Obviously the signature is a handwriting font, but you get the idea. Of course a handwritten signature would appear on an actual letter. There were no enclosures. You will notice the typist's initials given after Harold Carson's initials at the bottom. You won't need to know it since it is unusual for students have secretaries, but I put it in for information. OK, here's another example.

1492 Columbus Avenue
Colville, WA 99114

March 21, 2001

Casper Chamber of Commerce
1214 Front Street
Casper, WY 82609

Dear Sir or Madam:

Greetings from someone who would like to visit your fine area. Please send me any information that is available on the events in Casper during this coming May. My family and I plan to visit the area and will also need a list of accommodations and restaurants. We also like to camp at times, so a list of nearby campgrounds would be nice. Please also include any maps and brochures you think would be helpful.

If you have suggestions of various web sites that might be informative, I would be happy to check them out.

Again, please send whatever pamphlets and information sheets about the events and accommodations as well as maps and or directions. I will appreciate whatever you send.

Thank you,

Nancy Johnson

Nancy Johnson

Notes on the above: There was no letterhead this time. Also there was no personal contact, so note the generic salutation that was used. Note the block style, the proper spacing, and the brevity of the letter. It should be short and to the point; don't wander and beat around the bush. Both of the examples have been letters written for information. Let's have you write a letter for information.

ASSIGNMENT: LETTER FOR INFORMATION

Write a letter for information. Follow the block form. Write to a company inquiring about the availability of a given product. Direct it to Mr. Arnold Black, Sales Supervisor. Make up the company name and the address. Use your own return address and your own name. Decide on the product you are looking for. Have three short paragraphs in the body of the letter.

LETTER OF COMPLAINT

Not everything happens just the way we would like it to happen. Sometimes we receive poor service from a business; at other times we may have difficulty with a product or run afoul of the warranty somehow. You need to be able to write a decent letter of complaint. Below are some things to consider when writing a letter of complaint.

You need to be specific. If you had a problem with service, the date and time and the name of the person are very helpful to get the situation remedied. Define the problem as best you can. Don't make general statements; be specific. If you have a problem with a product, include as much information as you can: date purchased, guarantees, price paid, serial number, and so forth. Again the key is to be specific.

It is also helpful if you know what it will take to satisfy you regarding the complaint. Will you take a letter or apology? Do you want your money back? Will a replacement product do? It is good to suggest but not demand. Be as positive as possible.

Three paragraphs should do it. The first states your complaint. The second gives supporting details, and the third restates your case and suggests a remedy.

ASSIGNMENT: LETTER OF COMPLAINT

Write a letter of complaint. Follow the block form. Write to a company about a complaint you have, either with service or a product. Direct it to Ms. Shirley Wilson, Customer Service Department. Make up the company name and the address. Use your own return address and your own name. Have three short paragraphs in the body of the letter reflecting the suggestions given above.

ABC Cabinets
4840 Eagle Trail
Macedonia, OH 44056

October 22, 2001

Customer Service
Allied Tools, Inc.
18022 Fielder Blvd.
Cincinnati, OH 45251

Dear Sir or Madam:

In the past I have had a number of good experiences with your company. Unfortunately, a tool I purchased from you last spring has not performed as expected. The tool, a special jig for holding items going through a band saw, your SKU# 18-5551-02, seems to not be able to hold its adjustment for more than two or three cuts.

The adjusting screws do not seem to hold any setting for very long. I have attempted all sorts of remedies, but they just will not hold. Admittedly, there is some vibration with the saw, but that certainly is a known factor and certainly was taken into account by those who engineered this tool. In fact, your own advertising makes the claim that saw vibration should not affect the settings.

Either I have a defective item, or the design is simply not good. Hopefully it is the former. I like what the tool does, but the constant adjusting offsets the value of the tool. I would like to replace the tool I have for another just like it. Please advise how this can be done. Thank you for attending to this matter.

Sincerely,

Raleigh Branstad

Raleigh Branstad

Notes on the above: You will note Mr. Branstad does not have a letterhead, but he does include his business name in the heading. He identifies the tool and uses a SKU number. It would be better if he had given the exact date of purchase; in fact, a photocopy of his sales receipt would have been a nice enclosure. He does explain the problem and suggests a course of action.

COVER LETTERS

One letter you may well write will be a cover letter. Cover letters are sent along with something else. The cover letter often has something to do with getting a job or an appointment for an interview of some sort. It may also be a letter to introduce included brochures or something else.

The focus here will be on a cover letter to go with a resume. Resumes will be taken up after you finish the letters section. You will either be writing to someone you know or someone you don't. Someone you know can be almost anyone. Someone you know can be someone with whom you made some personal contact previous to the letter. Your contact might be as minimal as a single phone call, but you have the person's name and will have spoken with them and gotten their name. If there is someone you mutually know who has recommended the company to you, be sure to include that person's name in your letter.

Cases where you don't know someone in particular might arise when replying to blind advertisements where only an post office box is given. Another scenario is when you are relocating some distance to a new area and need a job when you get there.

The content of the cover letter varies somewhat depending on the situation, but the particular purpose of the cover letter is to accompany and introduce your resume. You may be trying to set up an interview, or you may be sending along the resume ahead of a scheduled interview. You might even be sending along an extra copy of your resume after a first interview just to keep your foot in the door.

Again, you should use the block style format. The entire cover letter should be one page only; three short paragraphs in the body will usually suffice. Paragraph one should contain an opening pleasantry and state the purpose, namely to introduce the resume. In the second paragraph you might mention something not found on the resume or explain something on the resume a bit more. The final paragraph should be only a sentence or two and indicate either an action you will take or one you with the reader to take.

Study the two examples of cover letters along with the notes on the following pages before you do the assignment below.

ASSIGNMENT: COVER LETTER

Write a cover letter. Follow the block form. Write to a company about an upcoming interview and mention your inclusion of a resume. Direct the letter to Mrs. June Foster, Human Resources. Make up the company name and the address. Use your own return address and your own name. Have three short paragraphs in the body of the letter reflecting the suggestions given above.

821 Orcas Drive
Minneapolis, MN 54312

July 23, 2001

Mrs. Helen Edwards
Human Resources
Falk, Blake & Company
5522 Armstead Avenue
Minneapolis, MN 54318

Dear Mrs. Edwards:

When Robert Mercer suggested I call you, I was unaware of the possibilities with your company. I've enclosed my resume to give you a better sense of my qualifications before we meet next Thursday for the interview. I am looking forward to meeting you in person and discussing future employment.

The resume does not state why I came to Minneapolis, and you might wish to know why. Last year my wife and I visited the area and found it quite attractive. We determined to commit ourselves to a move. My wife, being a teacher, was able to secure employment with one of the local schools, and we have since moved here. As you can see from my resume, I have tended to stay on and move up in the two previous companies at which I've been employed, and I would bring the same degree of commitment to your company.

Mrs. Edwards, I do look forward to meeting you in person this coming Thursday, particularly since you have been so helpful on the phone. I am excited about the possibility of working for Falk, Blake & Company.

Sincerely,

John M. Snyder

John M. Snyder

Notes on the above: He has a personal contact and uses the name well. He has an interview scheduled and refers to it and his eagerness to be a part of the company. The letter is courteous, informative, brief, and to the point. He introduced his resume.

1429 Greenbriar Street
Aberdeen, SD 57401

June 5, 2002

The Morning Sun
PO Box 3485-N
St. Louis, MO 63131

Dear Sir or Madam:

Since I am planning to relocate to St. Louis, your advertisement for a salesperson caught my interest. Your ad stated you were an expanding company, and I am interesting in becoming part of a growing company. My resume is included for your information.

You will note that I previously lived in St. Louis while in college. My desire is to work in a larger city, and I am already familiar with St. Louis. Additionally I have a brother who lives in St. Louis, so that is an added incentive to move there. You will find his number on the resume, so please call that number to reach me after June 10. On my resume you will also see that I have strong experience in sales.

I am excited about relocating to St. Louis and the possibility of gaining employment with your company. Sales are my strong point, and I am sure we could prosper together. I look forward to hearing from you after the tenth and certainly desire to speak with you about possible employment.

Sincerely,

Wilma Brown

Wilma Brown
Sales Associate

Notes on the above: Wilma uses her title below her name. She is answering a blind ad from the newspaper so has no personal contact; thus, she uses the generic salutation. The name of the newspaper is in italics. Wilma introduces her resume and gives a little side information. She mentions she is relocating anyway and will need a job but also has some previous contact with the community.

POLITICAL LETTERS

Not only is it your right, it is your duty to write to those who rule over you. Local, state, and national officials fall into this category. Most of the time you will write to elected officials. It is also the case that often you will write to express your opinion and ask for either support or a stand against a certain bill or issue.

As an aside, one of my friends worked for a congressman in Washington, D.C. This individual stated that only about one out of a thousand constituents ever wrote their congressman. Think of the influence one letter for or against something would have. Elected officials are very aware that public sentiment is important and that they need to be in the mainstream of that sentiment most of the time to get reelected. They do pay attention to letters.

If you are writing to a congressman or governor or some other elected official at the state or national level, you should include The Honorable in their title in the first line of the inside address. The person's full name follows it on the same line of the inside address. *The Honorable* can be abbreviated to *The Hon.* If you know their title, you can put it in before their name in the salutation: Dear Representative Grundy, Dear Senator Wicks, Dear Assemblywoman Turpin, Dear Governor Sheridan.

Once again you should be brief and to the point. If there is a particular bill you are speaking to, be sure to give its correct number and title. SB 532 or HB 929 are examples of senate bills or house bills. State your purpose in the first paragraph, give your compelling reasons in the second paragraph, and ask for a commitment of some sort in the third paragraph. Be courteous and respectful, but state your case clearly and emphatically.

Always remember that these elected officials are there to represent you and others. Don't threaten or belittle them. Compliment them when you can, and try to be positive. State your case clearly and succinctly, and make the best case you can for your position.

Study the example of the political letter that follows before you do the assignment below.

ASSIGNMENT: POLITICAL LETTER

Write a political letter. Follow the block form. Write to some elected official representing your area. Perhaps your teacher will provide some names and addresses. These will vary depending on where you live. Use your own return address and your own name. You can either make up an issue or bill or write an actual letter about a bill or issue that is current in your own area. Have three short paragraphs in the body of the letter reflecting the suggestions given above.

14977 Lower River Road
Grants Pass, OR 97526

September 18, 2001

The Honorable Edgar Willson
House Office Building
Room 207
Salem, OR 97305

Dear Assemblyman Willson:

Thank you for your representation of Southern Oregon. I do appreciate your past record of support for helping the agricultural interests in our area. Currently I am concerned about HB 482, the bill in your committee that would remove the lid on forest taxes. Certainly you can see what a negative effect on small woodlands owners this bill would have should it be passed. I am asking you to vote against HB 482.

Currently we small woodland owners pay taxes on the land but not on the trees until they are harvested. HB 482 would begin assessing us on an annual basis for the value in the trees as well as the land. In some cases this would necessitate harvesting the trees to pay the taxes. Trees are not like most other farm crops. We have to wait a long time between harvests. It seems only fair that we pay when we harvest since that is the time we realize a cash value from the crop.

Again, I ask you to oppose HB 482 for the sake of keeping the small woodlots growing in Southern Oregon. Thanks again for all you've done in the past. I hope to hear back from you on this issue, and I look forward to your vote against HB 482 while it is still in your committee.

Sincerely,

Robert Coursey

Robert Coursey

Notes on the above: The first line of the inside address could have read The Hon. Edgar Willson. Robert is courteous and thankful but firm. He states his case and gives a couple of reasons for his position. The letter is short and to the point. He asks for action, in this case a vote against HB 482.

THE RESUME

A resume is generally a summary of your personal history, usually job related, that you put onto one or two pieces of paper. A single page resume is best and will usually suffice for someone who is young and has limited experience. Your intent in the resume is to include everything that supports the fact that you can do a particular job well.

You should know some general things about resumes. First, they are not good job search tools. Don't think you can write up some generic sheet about yourself, make a hundred copies, and send it out to a hundred companies, and then expect to get job offers. Second, not all jobs will need a resume. If you get a job with a relative or family friend, you probably won't need a resume. Often entry level jobs or unskilled labor positions don't require a resume. However, it is better to have one than not.

Employers often ask for resumes. That's a good reason to have one. A good resume will help you set down your objectives and will also help you to do a self-evaluation. Taking an inventory of your skills and experience is a good thing. It helps you to better communicate your talents and abilities. A resume can also be a good entry tool to get an interview. Often businesses ask for resumes to look through before granting interviews. Resumes are used to screen out applicants.

Today everyone has some access to a computer. It may be at school, the library, your own home, or even a cyber café. With a computer it is easy to tailor resume for each specific job or company. Take advantage of the computer for this task. Use good quality paper, but keep it white, off-white, or a very light tan. Other colors are not recommended. One thing you need to be sure and do is to proofread the resume a number of times. One of my friends used to work in a major company in its human resources department. He would always ask for a letter of application and a resume. He would remove any applicant from the pool if he found a mistake on the letter or the resume. His reasoning was they just weren't careful folks. Take a lesson. Proofread your resume!

There are a variety of formats for resumes. In this book you will learn only one format. It is a design which came about during my tour as a teacher in an adult vocational school. This format works. Many of my former students were able to get interviews and jobs by using this format for their resumes. Follow it and adapt it for your purposes.

Your resume needs a header. It should start with your name. Center the header at the top of the page down the standard half inch or so. You should write your first and last name - (Alfred Brown). A middle initial is acceptable if you use it regularly or you have a very common name - (Richard V. Smith). If you go by your middle name, then write your first initial and your middle and last name - (T. William Sloan).

Skip one space between your name and the next line. The next two or three lines should include your address and a phone number where you can be reached. It is acceptable to include an e-mail address also. Use one or at the most two type faces in your resume. Times New Roman 12 point is generally the best, but you can use Arial for headings or your address and phone number. Your name should be in bold letters and perhaps enlarged to 14 or 16 point, but don't make it too large.

The first thing after the header is your objective statement. This needs to be tailored for each specific job and company. Avoid using a narrow job title, but don't be overly general either. If you know a specific opening is available and you want to try for that job, make the objective suit that job. Use an active verb. The objective should start with a capital letter and end with a period, but it doesn't have to be a complete sentence. It should be no longer than two lines on your resume. On the next page you will find a series of objective statements. Write down a few attempts and revise things until it feels right. This is the most important statement on your resume.

Sample Job Objectives

Seeking full time employment where my youth and vigor can be put to work assisting my employer for our mutual benefit.

To put my skills and abilities to work for A.K. Lasers, Inc. for the mutual benefit of the company, the clients, and myself.

To put my aptitude and experience to work as an electronic technician with Clackamas Communications for our mutual profit.

Seeking a responsible position with A-1 Financial requiring skills in public relations, writing and reporting.

Desire a position with Afco Sales where my past management and sales expertise can be put to work for our mutual benefit.

Aggressive and success-oriented professional seeking a sales position with Victory Company which offers both challenge and growth.

Competent and experienced office manager desires a similar position with Two Rivers Medical Clinic.

Your resume needs to present to your potential employer a series of reasons why the employer should hire you. The rest of your resume should make that point over and over again. The person reading your resume should get a quick picture of you, and that picture needs to contain certain things: your skills, experience, training, and accomplishments. Stop! Read those three sentences again. It's important.

The two items highest on the list in the minds of most employers are what you bring to the table in the way of skills and experience. Younger people often won't have much experience, but that is understandable because of age. Skills break down into two basic areas: personal and professional. Personal skills are things like getting along with others, being a good communicator, being a hard and efficient worker, able to manage people well, and so forth. The professional skills are those skills that are particularly job related: able to type 55 wpm, skilled with radio test equipment, can do layout and design work on the computer. You should have a section for both types of skills on your resume.

In my area, the local businesses were polled to see what they were looking for in people taking entry level jobs. More than 350 businesses responded. For personal skills the top ten items listed in order were the following: dependability, honesty, positive attitude, pleasant personality, communication skills, loyalty, tact, team-oriented, initiative, good grooming. Here's the list for professional skills: typing, filing, spelling/punctuation, office procedures, word processing, ten-key proficiency, composing letters, accounting, and business math. Note that these businesses were looking for people to work in offices.

You need to take an inventory of yourself. You are looking at yourself to see if you have good worker skills. Try to write down at least ten personal skills you have and then edit the list back to your seven or eight strongest skills. Do the same with a set of professional skills for yourself. Personal skills will adapt to most any job. Some professional skills might not apply to every job situation.

One of the best ways to come up with a list of skills is to think of jobs you have had, even short jobs. Think of what you did on those jobs. What you did represents skills you used to get through the job. Let's say you were called on by your service club to help in the concession stand at a series of local games. Did you have to work under pressure, handle money, be flexible, cook, meet customers, solve problems, and sell? All of these activities represent skills you put to work.

What about experience? Again, you have to think of what you have done and put those activities in a good light. What did you do that has some application or transfer to the job you are seeking? Maybe you trained or managed people in some capacity. Perhaps you did similar work to the job you are wishing to land. Think these things through. Let's say you delivered newspapers for a couple of years. The key is to couch the experience in good terms. Instead of saying you delivered newspapers, why not say that you operated and managed a delivery route. Think again of what you did on that route. Did you manage money and materials; did you have to deal with customer complaints? Were you dependable to get the papers delivered each day, and did you have a backup plan when you couldn't do it? The key is to be creative in your thinking.

Education is often found on resumes, but it is not necessary unless you need to fill the space or the schooling was job-specific. Often times the education question is covered on the job application itself.

Certainly you should have a section about your accomplishments. You all have them. Maybe you got an award. Perhaps you exceeded a quota or brought costs down or made things more efficient. You might have risen through the ranks quickly or been given extra responsibility not normally handed to a person of your age, position, or experience. Again, you need to do some thinking on this. Just because you did it, doesn't mean anyone else could have done it. One former student of mine had built up an Avon route of about 300 customers. She quit doing Avon to "take a real job" as she put it. The job she took was in a fast food place, and I'm not talking management. I asked her if she had sold her Avon route. It never entered her mind; she didn't think it was worth anything.

There are other categories you could place on your resume. A personal statement at the end may be appropriate. If you have experience and are a member of some professional organizations, that also might be a good thing to include. The key things, though, are your skills, experience, and accomplishments. They represent your potential to a future employer.

Remember, writing a good resume means you need to ask yourself a series of questions to get information about yourself. It is not a time to be humble. You want to put your best foot forward. Certainly you need to be honest but if you don't tell the job screener or employer, who will?

The format of the resume will be obvious in the examples. It is designed to make it easy to read. Just the design alone will be impressive since it shows care, thought, and organizational skills. Study the examples before doing the following assignment.

ASSIGNMENT: WRITE A RESUME

Follow the general format given in the examples. Have a heading and categories. Be careful to proofread your resume. Any spelling or punctuation error would be a real negative. Be creative but honest in your statements. Make your resume only one page in length. Go to the next page and answer the questions to generate information for your resume. Note: either *resume* or *resumé* is correct; this text uses the first spelling.

RESUME INFORMATION SHEET

What job am I attempting to find? If not a particular job, what line of work am I interested in?

Why do I want this type of job or this particular job?

Write an objective directed toward the job or field or company. Be as specific as possible.

Rate yourself on the following skills by circling the x in the proper column.

	normally	50/50	seldom
accept supervision	x	x	x
adaptable	x	x	x
get along with co-workers	x	x	x
meet deadlines	x	x	x
good attendance	x	x	x
hard worker	x	x	x
honest	x	x	x
organized	x	x	x
productive	x	x	x
punctual	x	x	x
quick learner	x	x	x
responsible/dependable	x	x	x

List two or three jobs you have had in the recent past.

Identify what you did on those jobs and translate that into a list of professional skills.

      job tasks   professional skills

List any accomplishments you can think of.

List any schooling or special training you have received.

List any job experience you have.

Donald B. Jackson

PO Box 828
Norton, VA 24273
(703) 679-1443

OBJECTIVE

To put my aptitude and experience to work as an electronic technician with Farsight Mobile Radio for our mutual profit.

PROFESSIONAL SKILLS

Repair and installation skills for many types of radio equipment
Service & trouble shooting skills on mobile units
Skilled with various radio test equipment
Experienced in all phases of repair
Experienced with mobile and base stations and repeaters

PERSONAL SKILLS

Excellent trouble shooting skills, intuitive thinker
Neat and well organized
Work well under pressure
Highly proficient at time management & scheduling, punctual
Work well with both co-workers and the public
Self-motivated and productive
Quick learner

EXPERIENCE

Eight years electronic technician for Motorola Service Center
Truck driver
Self-employed with business in twelve states

ACCOMPLISHMENTS

US Army, Vietnam veteran
Completed single engine rotor turbine helicopter mechanic course
Hundreds of thousands of miles long haul driver with no tickets or accidents

EDUCATION/TRAINING

Journeyman electronic technician
Commercial driver's license
One year of college education

PERSONAL STATEMENT

I have a strong desire to put my electronic skills and experience to work again so that my natural aptitudes can be developed for our mutual benefit.

Z. James Wimple

5253 Ambrose Way, Bakersfield, CA 93306
(805) 398-7310

OBJECTIVE

Seeking full time employment where my youth and vigor can be put to work assisting my employer for our mutual benefit.

EXPERIENCE

Heating, Ventilation & Air Conditioning experience
Oversaw household chemical department in a Wal-Mart store
Taught Spanish for IES Schools, 3-5th grades
Cook, general kitchen chores, and kitchen manager at The Wheel Inn
Casual forestry work: chainsaws, felling, bucking, cutting
Customer service for a national mail order house

PROFESSIONAL SKILLS

Type 50 wpm
Computer literate - long term experience with Microsoft Word
Able to run tractors with front loaders and other implements
Some small hand tool and power tool experience
Excellent phone skills

PERSONAL SKILLS

Get along well with people, able to work with most anyone
Able to manage & motivate people
Good sense of humor
Quick learner
Persistent
Good team player
Work hard to be efficient
Willing to ask questions and take instruction

ACCOMPLISHMENTS

Picked for the Oxford experience
Participated in forestry camp
Member National Junior Honor Society

BENEFITS TO EMPLOYER

Willing to learn your system and work hard
Highly motivated to do well and move into management
Eager to work with a young and growing company

EDUCATION

Bachelor of Arts degree in English from Central Valley College
Completed an exchange semester study at Keble College, Oxford, England

Frank Ellingsworth

2342 Old Mine Road
Dufur, OR 97021
(503) 297-8111

OBJECTIVE

Seeking full time employment with Safeway where my skills and talents in the grocery business may develop.

PERSONAL SKILLS

Dependable and disciplined
Meet deadlines well
Good communicator
Excellent memory skills
Organized and efficient worker
Quick learner
Adaptable yet content with routines
Proven ability to work well with others

PROFESSIONAL SKILLS

Able to organize jobs and time well
Good monetary and math skills
Confident with computer spreadsheets and data entry
Able to open and close daily accounts
Capable of setting up schedules for myself and others

EXPERIENCE

Part time help at Stop and Go Market for two summers
Ran a delivery route for three years
Cared for lawns and yards of various neighbors
Helped in school kitchen in food preparation

ACCOMPLISHMENTS

Picked as hardest worker in my senior class
Elected student of the month
Increased the customers on my delivery route by 24%

BENEFITS TO EMPLOYER

Have a strong desire to excel in the work place
Have positive relationships with many of the people in the area
Exhibit good values of punctuality, honesty, and hard work

EDUCATION

High School Diploma
Graduate of Toastmasters

SECTION 5

The Principle of Condensation

THE PRINCIPLE OF CONDENSATION

The name of this section is revelatory of the activity you are going to practice. Your job is to condense writings of various lengths. You will begin with some sentences and move to paragraphs and then to longer works. These exercises do not have right and wrong answers, but some answers are better than others. This section has some answer keys at the back of the book, but they are meant for direction only. You should look at the answers after you have written your own answers. What you will be checking for is to see if you have done something similar.

The principle of condensation is a process. Condensation is reducing, abridging, abbreviating, shortening, cutting, compressing, compacting, or distilling. It is the art of boiling down the idea to its bare bones, of cutting out the fat. Good papers are not padded; they are composed of muscle and bone, not fat. You have already seen how the seven sentences in a five paragraph essay form a skeleton. On the skeleton are placed the supporting details, the muscle of the argument. Extraneous ideas are like fat; they can be dropped without loss of meaning.

Not only will this principle help you in your writing, it will help you when doing research and taking notes. You should be able to capture the essence of an argument or idea in just a few words. Later you can utilize those notes in writing a paper full of good information, a paper that doesn't wander or beat around the bush. Good notes make writing a paper an easier job. Many was the night when I saw fellow students trying to write a paper with half a dozen books open in front of them alongside the typewriter. They sure looked busy, but in most cases it was copy a little from here and a little from there and hope that the jumble made some sense.

The exercises in this section are few, but the opportunity for further practice is myriad. Your teacher will probably assign at least three or four more articles to condense. A variation on the précis is to require an exact number of words in the finished product, always less than a third of the original. It is a challenge to reduce 170 words to 45 words exactly and still retain the flavor and thrust of the source piece. *Reader's Digest* is a great example of this type of writing since many of the articles and stories are condensed from the originals.

You will notice that answers to the basic questions of *who, what, where,* and *when* generally comprise the basic information. Answers to two other questions, *why* and *how,* provide most of the rest of whatever essential information is found. A short excerpt from Rudyard Kipling's *Just-So Stories* illustrates the above quite handily.

> I keep six honest serving men
>   (They taught me all I know);
> Their names are What and Why and When
>   And How and Where and Who.

Learn to digest the information you read and hear so that you can penetrate to the heart of the matter. When you write, be clear and concise; don't waste your reader's time. Have something to say. Read good material and take careful notes. Rarely should you copy unless the original says it with such punch that a paraphrase would dilute it to insufficiency.

THE PRINCIPLE OF CONDENSATION EXPLAINED

1. Discern the secondary material from primary ideas.

2. Reduce the physical length of the original.

3. Retain the order and logic of the elements.

4. Retain the essence (main points & spirit) of the original.

5. Drop the non-essential information and structures of the original.

Names applied to such condensations include *abstract, précis, summary, digest,* and *synopsis.*

THE SENTENCE

1. Drop repeated items.

2. Use vocabulary - change phrases to words.

    did not amount to much = insignificant

3. Change word classes of important words to tighten structure.

    The dog ran the coon up a tree. = The dog treed the coon.

THE PARAGRAPH

1. Identify the main point of the paragraph.

2. Decide if supporting information confirms the main point.

3. Handle as a précis or write a single summary sentence of 15 words or less.

THE ESSAY, CHAPTER, ARTICLE

1. Pay particular attention to the first and last paragraphs.

2. Identify the central thesis and conclusion.

3. Write a one sentence summary (15 words or less) of each body paragraph as you read through it.

4. Write your condensation from your notes.

WORD ECONOMY EXERCISE #1

DIRECTIONS: Each of the following contains unnecessary words; rewrite each sentence in a shorter form.

1. Turn right when you come to the corner of State Street.

2. He did his work in a manner that showed he didn't care.

3. The Chihuahua is a type of dog that has no hair.

4. Bluebeard was a monster without a heart, without a soul.

5. He approaches all his problems in a manner like that of a child.

6. The tiny, little kitten is certainly a sight to behold.

7. The car crawled up the hill at a pace resembling a snail.

8. When you speak, put emphasis on the most important words and ideas.

9. Words that are not necessary should be cut out of your writing.

10. It is your duty to correct statements which are wrong.

11. They bought a horse that no one can manage.

12. The girl who is wearing the red hat is my cousin.

13. Your conduct at the dance was such that it shocked everyone.

14. It was a warm, romantic evening, full of moonlight.

15. If it could talk, that house which is on 92nd street might reveal many secrets.

16. Without making any noises, we entered the house which was darkened.

17. He opened the door with a smile that seemed to welcome us.

18. He always has a manner that is very cheerful.

19. The old man, who didn't have a penny, refused to accept my gift.

20. This tool has many uses to it.

21. I spent the night in a warehouse that was infested with rats.

22. The news, which startled us, made us change our plans in a way that was abrupt.

23. He likes his coffee without any sweetening in it.

24. This test is filled with beauty.

25. Though he is a recent immigrant from a foreign country, he speaks English without a trace of an accent.

WORD ECONOMY EXERCISE #2

_____ Name

DIRECTIONS: Each of the following contains unnecessary words; rewrite each sentence in a shorter form.

1. Manners of the best sort are needed when with good company.

2. His redundancy was obvious as he repeated the cliché over and over.

3. I had a bad attack of insomnia last night, and I was unable to sleep.

4. The consensus of opinion is that we should have a daily rehearsal every day for the next two weeks.

5. The first broadcast of the play on the air was its premiere on 16 December at 10 p.m. in the evening.

6. It is clearly evident that we must operate immediately without delay.

7. Unfortunately, we arrived during the season when it rains most of the time.

8. Tony is a pianist who is very talented.

9. The medal was awarded to him posthumously after his death.

10. She turned her sad, unhappy face to me and spoke in a tired, dreary voice.

11. I can remember back to the day when I liked nothing but jazz music exclusively.

12. The desire for admiration is a universal craving possessed by all people.

13. As soon as he has finished, he will call you.

14. It isn't difficult to make your home modern.

15. When the storm broke, the golfers hurriedly broke for shelter.

16. After he settled in New Jersey, John became a stingy miser and lived alone in solitude all by himself.

17. The women of America spend millions of dollars annually in an effort to make themselves beautiful.

18. My Aunt Tillie sent me a tie that had been painted by hand; it was a Christmas gift.

19. In order to play better, you'll have to practice more often.

20. Some people were eating peanuts while the play was going on.

21. Hitler was a man completely lacking in mercy.

22. Your decision is one that is not just.

THE PRÉCIS

A brief summary of the main points of an article is called a *précis*. In such a composition, which should be not more than one-third as long as the original, your job is to express the central idea of the original writer in clear, concise language of your own. All illustrations, amplifications, or embellishments are omitted from the précis; it includes only the bare essentials.

The following are a few simple rules for making a précis:

1. Read the original through attentively to learn the general idea.
2. Read it a second time, looking up all unknown words, phrases or allusions. This time you judge the selection
   more carefully by differentiating what appears to be important versus what is detail.
3. List in your own words what you judge to be the essential point or points made by the author.
4. Write the first draft of your précis; omit examples, illustrations, conversations, or any repetitions.
5. Read your first draft and compare it with the original for accuracy and emphasis.
6. Eliminate all unnecessary words and change words until you have expressed concisely and clearly what you
   believe to be the main point of the selection.

EXAMPLE

What are the real aims of study? The object of study is, in the first place, to get fast and firm possession of facts--facts of spelling, reading, mathematics, composition, history, language, geography, and the like. It is highly desirable that we should know how to spell *Chicago* and *business*, *Boston* and *brains*, and that we should know for all time. We want to know once and for all that seven times nine are sixty-three, that Abraham Lincoln signed the Emancipation Proclamation, that an island is a body of land completely surrounded by water, and that a proper name should begin with a capital letter. Many, many, minute facts as well as certain connected bodies of truth should be embedded in one's memory as deeply and securely as a bullet that has lodged in the heart of a growing tree. Also one should master certain processes of though and grip a few great underlying and unchanging principles of life and conduct. (160 words)

ANALYSIS

After a careful reading of the above, three distinct thoughts surface:
1. The first aim of study is to acquire facts; many examples are given.
2. The second aim is to master processes of thought.
3. The third aim is to learn certain principles of conduct and life.

Thus, a first draft might look something like this: There are three aims of studying: to learn the necessary facts in many areas, to learn how to think, and to learn great rules about life and the conduct of it. (32 words)

Since the above is still wordy, pare a bit more of the fat, and the précis might resemble the following: The aims of study are three: to acquire needed facts, to learn how to think, and to learn the universal principles of life and conduct. (25 words)

That's how it's done, and you can do it. The aim is to reduce the verbiage while still making the point and retaining some of the flavor or spirit of the original. There are no single right answers to these kinds of exercises. You will need to think a bit and be careful in your choice of words, but the skill of condensing information is very valuable and will serve you well in the future.

EXERCISES IN THE ART OF PRÉCIS WRITING #1

DIRECTIONS: Write a précis for each of the following; make sure your piece is one-third or less than the length of the original. A word count is given for your convenience at the end of each passage. Your three summaries should be on a separate sheet of paper.

1) An alert and curious man goes through the world taking note of all that passes under his eyes and collects a great mass of information which is in no sense incorporated into his own mind but remains a definite territory outside his own nature, which he has annexed. A man of receptive mind and heart, on the other hand, meditating on what he sees and getting its meaning by the divining rod of the imagination, discovers the law behind the phenomena, the truth behind the fact, the vital force which flows through all things, and gives them their significance. The first man gains information; the second gains culture. The pedant pours out an endless succession of facts with a monotonous uniformity of emphasis and exhausts while he instructs; the man of culture gives us a few facts, luminous in their relation to one another, and freshens and stimulates by bringing us into contact with ideas and life. (157 words; yours should be 52 or less)

2) It is dangerous to assume that our country's welfare belongs alone to that mysterious mechanism called the government. Every time we allow or force the government, because of our own individual or local failures, to take over a question that properly belongs to us, by that much we surrender our individual responsibility, and with it a comparable amount of individual freedom. But the very core of what we mean by Americanism is individual liberty founded on individual responsibility, equality before the law, and a system of private enterprise that aims to reward according to merit. (95 words; yours should be 32 or less)

3) What is the matter with our reading is our casualness, languor, preoccupation. We don't give the book a chance. We don't put ourselves at the disposal of the book. It is impossible to read properly without using all one's engine power. If we are not tired after reading, common sense is not in us. How should one grapple with a superior and not be out of breath? But even if we read with the whole force of our brain, and do nothing else, common sense is still not in us, but sublime conceit is. For we are assuming that without further trouble, we can possess, co-ordinate, and assimilate all the ideas and sensations rapidly offered to us by a mind greater than our own. The assumption has only to be stated in order to appear in its monstrous absurdity. Hence it follows that something remains to be done. This something is the act of reflection. Reading without subsequent reflection is ridiculous; it is equally proof of folly and vanity. (169 words; yours should be 56 or less)

EXERCISES IN THE ART OF PRÉCIS WRITING #2

DIRECTIONS: Write a précis for each of the following; make sure your piece is one-third or less than the length of the original. A word count is given for your convenience at the end of each passage. Your three summaries should be on a separate sheet of paper.

1. That man, I think, has had a liberal education who has been so trained in youth that his body is the ready servant of his will and does with ease and pleasure all the work that as a mechanism it is capable of; whose intellect is a clear, cold, logic engine to be turned to any kind of work and spin gossamers as well as forge the anchors of the mind; whose mind is stored with a knowledge of the great and fundamental truths of nature and of the laws of her operations; one who, no stunted ascetic, is full of life and fire but whose passions are trained to come to heel by a vigorous will, the servant of a tender conscience; one who has learned to love all beauty, whether of nature or of art, to hate all vileness and to respect others as himself. Such a one, and no other, I conceive, has had a liberal education, for he is, as completely as a man can be, in harmony with nature. He will make the best of her and she of him. They will get on together rarely, she as his over-beneficent mother, he as her mouthpiece, her conscious self, her minister and interpreter. (255 words; reduce to 80 or less)

2. While the technical structure of developmental reading may be a more efficient means for meeting the limited goals of competency testing, its restriction of overall language experience can only be construed as inefficient means for producing mature readers able to cope with the complexities of real language. To deny the full linguistic, aesthetic and cognitive experience of literary study to students, and instead to offer them the restricted and restricting experience of developmental reading exercises is truly a waste of our time as English teachers. The rejection of technical rationality to the English curriculum does a greater service to the community in terms of personal growth and freedom than the application of technical rationality to the English curriculum does in raising of competency test scores. Our faith in machinery is beginning to take precedence over our faith in the abilities of our students; by the 1990's language arts may be replaced by language engineering. (153 words; reduce to 50 or less)

3. The rise of the fortunes of biblical theology within evangelicalism has served to help preserve the dialogue concerning the proper relationship of Law and Gospel as well as the utility of the Mosaic law for the contemporary Christian. There are a multitude of key ancillary issues that are generated by the Law/Gospel question, such as the purpose of the Mosaic law in the Old Testament and Paul's treatment of the law. Indeed, this important complex of concerns has been the subject of numerous books in recent years. This fact serves to confirm the importance of the issue for the Christian church and underscores the fact that there is no consensus of understanding of the relationship between Law and Gospel. Differing systems of theology often have radically different conceptions of the proper relationship between Law and Gospel. Since one's understanding of these issues has a direct impact on the application of the life of the believer in Christ, I believe it is imperative and helpful to decide the proper relationship of Mosaic law to the saint. (175 words; reduce to 58 words or less)

PARAGRAPH CONDENSATION

The object here is to reduce each paragraph of the following article to a short sentence expressing a single idea. A phrase or some other string of words is also acceptable for your own notes, but write a single sentence for each summary in this exercise. The basic point of the paragraph in your estimation is what you want. You should express it in your own terms, and it will probably differ somewhat from the key or what others might write. The goal is to be in general agreement about the basic idea; the expression of the idea is your own. There are twenty paragraphs in the article. Number your sentences to correspond with the paragraphs.

This article appeared a newspaper, the *Santa Ana Register*, on February 28, 1982. The author, Van Wilkinson, taught English at the time at Victor Valley High School in California. His article had previously appeared in *The High School Journal*, a publication of the University of North Carolina at Chapel Hill.

This article is just a sample. Any short article from a magazine or pieces of suitable length from newspapers or newsletters can be used for practice. Even short sections from non-fiction books can be utilized. Mastering this technique will be of immense help when writing larger papers. In that case, you will probably be putting your individual sentences on note cards instead of writing them on a single sheet of paper.

"Sports Rule the Mind"

1) It is Monday, before class, in early March. I am reviewing my roll sheets and grade book, the roll sheets in particular. There is a school list of last Friday's absentees. In my five high school English classes of about 30 students each, there were 27 students absent that day--three were sick, one was truant, two did not appear on the list, and the other 21 were excused to participate in sports. There was a test Friday; there was also an essay due. It would take me an extra two hours or so to arrange makeups. Then it would start again. Tuesday I would lose six or seven to baseball, the same on Thursday, and Friday, if the basketball team was still in the playoffs and the track meet was not rained out, another 21. Since these teams had to travel much of the time, they were missing school sometimes half a day, to sit on a bus.

2) With a little calculation I tallied the lost curricular hours. In an average week during seasonal peaks, 35 curricular hours were lost, mostly in my afternoon classes. Then there was the time I would spend trying to coordinate makeups. Some weeks were much better, but I could find none in which less than 15 curricular hours were lost. More calculations. In a 36-week school year, it averaged around 22 hours per week, or 792 curricular hours--enough time to sent one student to class for almost nine semesters--4½ years--in my classes alone!

3) Before I could dabble further in amateur statistics, the day custodian came to tell me that there would not be any classroom cleanup until Wednesday; the night shift custodians were too busy cleaning the stadium, rearranging the gymnasium, and servicing the locker rooms. He did, however, tell me the good news: They would fix the two cracked windows in my room next month--after the maintenance crew finished refurbishing the weight room and repairing the sprinklers out on the athletic fields. I thanked him and stared at my 792 hours figure.

4) More calculations: A team athlete averaged about four curricular hours lost per week during competition, which continued most of the year for multi-team participants. At four hours a week for a semester, it could easily amount to 72 hours, or 12 full school days. And that athlete usually put in a couple of hours per day, on average, practicing or competing. That added another 10 hours per week or 180 hours per semester. All in all , a team athlete could be committing about 252 hours per semester to one sport, or the equivalent of 42 full school days, time inarguably void of curricular studies. And I was not even guessing at the "tired time" an athlete lost afterward, arriving home too bushed to bother.

5) The figures outlined a menacing specter. But it had to wait. After I talked briefly with two of the hurried night shift custodians and glanced through our school's budget, a new jumble of statistics revealed a pitiful blight. Depending on how I deciphered the budget, somewhere between 15 and 25 percent of all custodial and maintenance costs were linked to after-school team athletics. Over half of the overtime pay for cleanup was due to staging athletic contests. Bookkeeping and secretarial services were harder to pin down, but it appeared as if the equivalent of one whole clerical position and one half an administrative "athletic director" position were needed to handle extracurricular athletic arrangements. Of course, transportation costs were beyond my logic. for every mile in curricular travel (e.g., field trips), the athletes traveled some nine miles. It cost $150 (a classroom set of paperbacks) per hour to run the stadium lights. And on it went, a tangle of substantial costs--all directly related to athletics--interwoven in the budget.

6) Amidst the weedy and often malnourished garden of public secondary education, there stands the sports orchard. It is handsomely looked after, even in hard times. Its roots reach under the garden and drain away nutrients. Visitors remark, "My, how the lettuce has stunted, but just look at those apples!" And the tax reformers, with a keen axe sharpened for school funding, swing on. Perhaps, but only perhaps, the orchard will fall to these axemen before they look up form their work to see how much has been leveled. And, as a curricular member of the long-wilted garden used to leftovers, getting extra-curricular team athletics out of public education will be a desirable side effect of the tax revolt.

7) The purpose of public secondary education, until 50 years ago, was to prepare adolescents curricularly for jobs and higher education. Athletics meant physical fitness and casual intramural games. In the intervening years, metamorphoses yielded the current quasiprofessional athletic establishment which, in effect if not in fact, dominates virtually every comprehensive secondary high school and many junior highs. When I voiced this observation to my school's principal, and ex-football coach and high muckety-muck in the state's athletic organization, he looked up from the sports page of the newspaper just long enough to say, "Yeah, it's no wonder. In this state, more coaches become administrators than any other group. You wouldn't want some literary type running a school like this would you?"

8) But tax cutters and critics of public secondary education are closing in on their own sacred ground. School boards, faced with decreasing enrollment, can cut only so deep into the "basics" of education before being compelled to face the hardest truth of the 1980's: public secondary schools will no longer be able to subsidize extracurricular athletics. Hurrah! Maybe they never should have.

9) Coaches and other indignant readers will have, by now, concocted sufficient contradictory data to dismiss my position as myopic, if not unpatriotic. I can hear them now: "Without athletic teams, school attendance will drop." "Athletics teaches responsibility and leadership." "Lots of kids go to college on athletic scholarships." "The community will always support extracurricular sports." Let us take these apart, one by one.

10) "Without athletic teams, school attendance will drop." Sure it will. The hangers-on who only show up to compete in sports will stop coming, and the schools will lose a lot of losers right then. The resultant change in the mood and the emphasis of the school will be well worth the brief and minor enrollment loss, as attention turns again to getting the academic material mastered instead of, "Who won the big one last Wednesday?" Those athletes who are also decent classroom performers (and some are) will not stop coming. There will be no riots, just fewer pep assemblies. In three years, most students will not notice the elimination of the school-sponsored sports scene. Many of the academically gifted and talented students, now relegated to obscurity and subjected to campus alienation, will rejoice at the change.

11) "Athletics teaches responsibility and leadership." Absolutely. So do classes in American history, drama, literature, science, psychology, and scores of other curricular offerings. So will physical education classes, in which teachers will once again have a fairly representative cross section of all students, not just those unfortunates who don't engage in team athletics. The "responsibility and leadership" ploy, incidentally, avoids the issue of all of the negative habits that team athletes are prone to develop: arrogance, indifference to academics, hypertrophy, reliance on team (collective) reinforcement, and convergent thinking.

12) "Lots of kids go to college on athletic scholarships." Quite right. But how many of them had to sacrifice a solid curricular background for the shot of it, and what of those who counted on it but just missed it? How many high school graduates go on to earn a living in athletics? Of students who go to college on athletic versus academic awards, which group tends to finish college? How many of these "athletic scholarships" are flimsily cloaked work/study contracts? (You work for the college as part of the team "company," and you can sort of study between workouts. Witness the recent plethora of college scholarship scandals and records alterations.) Somehow, the scholastic credibility of athletes on scholarships holds little luster. Besides, why should a fine-tuned body alone earn someone a spot in an institution of higher *learning*, especially if that spot displaces an otherwise qualified non-jock? In short, public funds should go to preparing students to go to the college of their choice by means of their brains, not their biceps.

13) "The community will always support sports." You bet they will--as long as they're subsidized by tax dollars. It's an easy ride, particularly for parent supporters. Your child is trained at no direct cost, enjoys the use of expensive equipment and facilities at no direct cost, and frequently is given special campus privileges in the process. Then, the school provides the parents with a low-cost or no-cost seat to enjoy the show. Of course the community supports it; it is dirt cheap. But it is only cheap because somewhere else curricular expenses have been throttled back to keep those teams out there as a public relations tool. The cogent question is: will the community support all of this if the costs are directly passed on to the "consumers" as in free enterprise?

14) That last question brings me to the thesis. If the wild-swinging tax revolters had a way to cut public secondary school costs by 20 percent, increase students' academic performance, and give the private sector legions of new businesses, would they not cry "love" and drop their axes? Sure they would, and here is how. Simply divorce public schools from athletic competition contrivance, and make it an entirely private free enterprise. Schools will rent out facilities; coaches will set up sports clubs for competition; schools will become athletically unburdened and scholastically rededicated. In many places where schools have gotten out of the driver training game, private driving schools, usually staffed after hours by ex-driver education teachers, do the job quite nicely. Let us do the same with team athletics.

15) When this conversion is made, and it will be made, the circle will be complete. Secondary education will have gone back to its rightful birthspot: the place to prepare adolescents curricularly for jobs and higher education. It students want to do it big in sports, they will do it on a private, separate, business basis. Free enterprise freaks will celebrate; school boards will have smaller but more academically effective budgets, augmented further by income from subletting facilities and manpower; teachers who coach will have a wider chance at earning additional income; and team competition will continue for the truly dedicated athlete.

16) If, as coaches of the nation maintain, athletic team competition is such a valuable part of a student's education, then it should be roundly and profitably supported after school hours on a business basis. If, on the other hand, sacrificing the current cozy arrangement results in a reduction in participation, then the total worth of athletic team competition will undergo its deserved devaluation. Let the sports orchard thrive or wither on its own merits, not on revenue channeled away from the scholastic, basic, curricular program.

17) Other improvements of consequence will follow the sportskill. For one, secondary schools will be free to hire subject matter teachers whose qualifications need not include coaching. At present, scarcely a secondary school opening on a small or medium sized campus does not require some extracurricular coaching. Often, individuals are hired for their supposed coaching ability, with only cursory attention being given to their academic competence. It is no wonder that students in these teachers' classes often remark, "I didn't learn anything about math, but I can name the defensive line of the Pittsburgh Steelers all the way back to 1971."

18) Another positive spin-off will be a renaissance in fundamental, academic teaching. The "back-to-basics" crusaders will be overjoyed. Free from the domination of tax-supported athletic showmanship, schools will start to refocus on the students' scholastic needs, and all those lost curricular hours will be recouped. The school day will be able to be shortened, if desired, with no loss in student achievement. On a per day basis, schools will stay free from the disruption of extracurricular athletic spectacles and hence be more able to concentrate on subject matter. And, yes, the physical education classes will flourish, with long-term physical fitness and health studies becoming priorities instead of collective competition. After all, if a student is taught to stay fit by working out on the team, what is he going to do when he is out of school and there is no team? Answer: ask all the overweight and middle-agers who made it big on their high school teams.

19) Critics of my tirade are wont to dismiss it with, "Aw, those academic teachers are just jealous. Their classes are so boring compared to athletics that they can't face it." A superficial survey would probably convey this--really, how can a discussion of the War of 1812, rhomboids, of denouement, or of democracy rival the snap and grit and exertion of team competition? It cannot. *It is not supposed to.* And that is the central point of the problem. Whenever

secondary schools promulgate policies allowing extracurricular athletics to stand on an equal footing with academics, the adolescent nature of students making choices will yield conclusive evidence that coaches are, in the main, more successful with students than classroom teachers. But consider: How successful would classroom teachers be if their students had to compete for a place on the roll sheet? How successful would classroom teachers be if the teacher had the authority to "cut" unproductive students from the class. And how successful would classroom teachers be if school administrations provided an elaborate public relations support system plus generous student rewards for participation in "classroom competition?"

20) The invitation is clear. All tax revolters, "back-to-basics" fanatics, and detractors of public secondary schools are welcome! Bring, and swing your axes! Chop away at the fat. If you hack long enough, the sports orchard will get its final pruning. Federal and state laws require an even bigger bite of school resources to the handicapped, to the "special education" segment. Where, in a fixed or diminishing school district budget does one look for those extra resources? You guessed it: anywhere but the sports orchard. So, when America finally bites the bullet, ending tax-backed extracurricular team competition, and makes it a separate, private endeavor, the withering curricular garden, which incidentally is saddled with training 90 percent of all students, will be in a better position to recapture needed funds and prestige.

SECTION 6

Major Papers

MAJOR PAPERS

You will find a variety of items in this section of the book. All of them will have something to do with writing a major paper. A major paper generally is at least a 1000 words in length. It is a work of research or opinion or combination of the two. Another name is the position paper; the paper states or clarifies a particular position regarding some subject. These papers should always be informative and may be persuasive as well.

Certain attributes of major papers are rather universal: title pages, references, and citations of some sort. The actual styles of these elements will vary according to the teachers, schools, and disciplines with which you must deal. Huge books, such as *The Chicago Manual of Style*, are devoted to all the intricacies of the finished product. The Modern Language Association used to, and perhaps still does, publish a booklet entitled *The MLA Style Sheet*. The scope of this chapter is to simply introduce you to the basic elements of a major paper and give you some simple guidelines for putting those elements together.

In this chapter you will learn about title pages, appendices, works cited pages, in text citations, and endnotes. You will also learn how to utilize note cards while doing the research and writing of your paper. The condensation techniques practiced in the previous chapter come into heavy play here. There is also a general overview of the procedures necessary for creating a major paper.

Your job will be to create a series of papers of at least 1000-1200 words. Each time you write a paper, some new element will be added so that you can practice putting the papers together. The procedure is incremental. You may have some latitude in picking your topics, or your teacher may simply assign them. You will find some check sheets for the major paper at the back of the book; look them over so that you will know what is expected of you on these papers.

A former student of mine went on to become a technical writer for Boeing. He said his job was to write technical papers and manuals. His engineering degree got him the job, but his writing skills enabled him to perform it. He said in effect that after learning how to write the 1200 word papers, the books he wrote now were just more of the same but bigger. Once mastered, these writing techniques can be adapted to a variety of tasks no matter what the size or occasion.

Examples of certain pages are given. Study these along with the explanation sheets so that you will be sure to get the correct form. The criteria given in the explanations and the samples will enable you to produce your own pages in the correct format. Spacing, punctuation, and alphabetical order are all important. When doing these pages, **you need to have an eye for detail**.

Using a computer for writing will greatly simplify your task in that the changes can be made without having to retype the whole page. If possible, secure the use of a computer, or at least one of the newer typewriters that has a memory and will retain your work. A typed paper or one generated from a computer printout is much easier for your teacher to read, and the neatness will help the overall effect of your paper.

On the next page you will find some general information regarding major papers and some specifics regarding the title page, an example of which follows on page 118. Please note that a title page has no number; the number 118 is the page number for this book, not the title page.

ORDER OF MAJOR PAPERS, TITLE PAGE & NUMBERING

The items below are given in the order of appearance when found in major papers.

 a) Title Page
 b) Text of paper
 c) Content Endnotes Page
 d) Appendix
 e) Works Cited Page (Bibliography)

THE TITLE PAGE

1. The purpose of the title page is to give the title of the paper, identify yourself as the author, and provide the date and other class information.

A) Provide balanced margins of two inches for all sides of the title page. (left, right, top, bottom)

B) The established order of items is
 1) title of the work,
 2) full name of author, and
 3) course information and date.

C) In the title follow these conventions:
 1) use capital letters and lowercase letters where appropriate;
 2) don't use a period or other end punctuation at the end;
 3) don't use quotes or underlines unless citing another title, and
 4) use double spaces between lines if more than one line is needed.

D) In the author area do the following:
 1) center these two lines in the middle of the page;
 2) place the word *by* on the first line;
 3) double-space and put your first and last name on the next line.

E) In the bottom third of the page place the following information in three lines.
 1) name of the course   **Format Writing**   * See the sample on
 2) name of the instructor   **Mr. Jensen**   the next page for
 3) the due date of the paper   **March 10, 1992**   the correct spacing.
 4) Double-space* and center all lines.

NOTE: In many cases the course hour, period, or section would be included along with the name of the course. Such information would be on the same line as the course name, would follow the course name, and would be separated by a comma from the course name.   **Writing 101, Section 106c**

PAGE NUMBERING

 1) There is no page number on the title page.
 2) All other pages are numbered beginning with the number 1; place the number in the top right hand corner against the right margin and one-half inch down from the top. Your last name can appear in front of the page numbers starting with 2, **Jensen 2**. Triple-space down from the page number to start the text.

A Correct and Proper Title Page

by

Ima Student

English 1A, Section 5

Mrs. Readypen

October 14, 1994

THE WORKS CITED PAGE

There are two basic areas where the works cited will appear, in the text and on the Works Cited page. The Modern Language Association (MLA) has established a standard style for the Works Cited page. Their version of the rules are below. The importance of listing the works you have cited in your paper is so that others who may have an interest can check your sources for further information. A standard methodology has evolved in which certain information is listed in a particular fashion so that others can most easily find their way back to the original document.

The advent of electronic storage and media has added some extras to the pre-existing system set up for standard printed material. The basic idea is still most important: does the information given allow the reader to find the original source with ease? The information given below lists a variety of principles, some general and some specific. Use these principles and the sample works cited page that follows as a reference. Note the formats, the elements included, and the punctuation.

1. Only the works which are actually cited in the paper are to be included on the Works Cited page. A Bibliography would include works which relate to the subject but were not used in the actual report.

2. Utilize the bibliography note cards to prepare the Works Cited page. Since you can shuffle the cards, the order will be easy to establish. All the necessary information should appear on the note cards.

3. Place the words *Works Cited* one inch down from the top of the page and centered. Double space between it and the first entry.

4. Arrange all items in alphabetical order according to the surname (last name) of the author. If no author is listed, then use the first important word of the title.

5. Place the first line of each entry flush with the left margin (usually an inch in). Indent all succeeding lines five spaces. Double space between all lines; that means between entries and lines within entries.

6. The following items are in order and are used for references about books. All items are not necessary except numbers 1, 3, and 8. Those three must always be included.

1) author(s)	6) number of volumes
2) chapter or part of book	7) name of the series
3) title of the book	8) place, publisher, date
4) editor, translator, compiler	9) volume number of this book
5) edition	10) page numbers

7. For journal and magazine articles use the following order omitting any unnecessary items:

1) author	3) name of the periodical
2) title of the article	4) volume, issue, and page numbers

8. Use a three-dash line with a period after it if there are two or more books by the same author.

9. For two or three authors of the same book, give the first author by surname, first name; do the rest with normal first name last name sequence. If there are more than three authors, use *et al* to refer to them.

10. Note how the items on the sample page that follows are punctuated. Book titles, magazine titles, and newspaper names are italicized; if you cannot italicize, use an underline instead. Article titles are in quotes. Pay special note as to how periods, commas, and colons are used.

11. See the sample page that follows for personal letters and interviews.

12. Electronic sources add any of the following as necessary.

      1) publication medium (CD, On-line, etc.)   3) path used to reach the information
      2) source of medium (WWW, URL...)   Protocol, Directory, Filename
                                                             4) date of access

For the present, CD-ROMs and the World Wide Web will probably be the most commonly used sources. For CD-ROMs, treat them pretty much as books or encyclopedias while making sure to add the first item above.

Web pages are a different situation, and things are still in flux. Various web sites and news pages offer their own challenges. Just be sure to cite how to get to them and when you went there. In the case of a news posting, you should use the date of the post, not the date you accessed it.

Obviously the information above dealing with electronic media will undergo some refinement in the future as things settle out and various authorities publish their versions of how to document such media. As a student, your best bet is to ask your teachers what they want in the way of documentation and then follow the guidelines they provide. Their way will be the accepted way at that particular time and place. Again, the most important idea is that someone else can trace back your information to the original source and can access that source correctly with as little trouble as possible. Think of it this way: if I gave you a quote from a book but did not include the page number, you would not easily find that quote, assuming you even bothered to look. The same goes for electronic media, especially the web. If the path is clear, someone else can follow it. Be clear, and be complete. That's the best advice I can give.

Works Cited

The Bible. Revised Standard Version.

Bulfinch, Thomas. *Bulfinch's Mythology*. 2 vols. New York: Mentor, 1962.

Campbell, Joseph. *The Hero With a Thousand Faces*. Cleveland: Meridian, 1956.

---. *The Masks of God*. New York: Viking, 1970.

"Fraud in the S&L Business." *Medford Mail Tribune* 22 Aug. 1986: D5.

Laird, Charles. "A Nonhuman Being Can Learn Language." *College Composition and Communication* 23

    (1972): 142-154.

Lopresto, Vince. interviewed by Ima Student. 1850 Carton Way, Murphy, OR. 25 Oct. 1992.

Mannheim, Max A. "Monkeys." *The World Book Encyclopedia*. 1976 ed.

Nordstrom, William, and Peter Brueler. *Saving for the Future*. Englewood Cliffs: Prentice, 1975.

Procter, David O., et al. *Multiplying Your Money*. New York: McGraw, 1980.

"Prosperity." *American Heritage Dictionary*. *Microsoft Bookshelf*. 1993 ed. CD-ROM. Redmond, WA:

    Microsoft, 1994.

"Saving or Investing." *Nation's Business* Apr. 1984: 22-24.

Smith, John. "John's Page: Good Marketing Tactics" at http://www.stateu.edu/users/jsmith/, 10 July 1996.

Smith, Robert, local Lutheran pastor. letter to Ima Student. 15 Mar. 1993.

"Thomas Jefferson." *Encyclopedia Americana*. 1982 ed.

Wicher, Lowell. "The New Bull Market." *Newsweek* 6 Sept. 1985: 19-23.

Zempe, Adrian. "They Took My Money." Letter to the Editor. *Grants Pass Daily Courier* 22 Jan.

    1988: A4, cols. 2-3.

WORKS CITED PRACTICE PAGE

DIRECTIONS: Prepare a works cited page using the 6 cards from the card catalog and the 7 items from the *Reader's Guide* excerpt. The *Reader's Guide* uses some abbreviations for magazine titles; full titles for those items are as follows: *Technology Review, U. S. News and World Report, Rolling Stone*, and *Science Digest*.

Reader's Guide section

card catalogue samples

ENERGY conservation

See also

Buildings--Heating and ventilation

Drilling for oil and gas in our houses. R. H. Williams and M. H. Ross. bibl il Tech R 82: 24-36 Mr/Ap '80

No shortage of ideas to solve energy crisis. ill U.S. News 88:70-1 My 12 '80

ENERGY policy

See also

Petroleum laws and regulations

Barry Commoner [Citizen's Party; interview by L. Weschler] B. Commoner. pors Roll Stone p44-8 My 1 '80

Charting our energy future: progress or prudence? [adaptation of address] E. Cook. il por Futurist 14:64-9 Ap '80

International aspects

See also

International Energy Agency

Brazil

Elasticity Snaps [gasoline price hike] N. Gall. il Forbes 125:59-60 Ap 28 '80

China

China updates ancient energy--with emphasis on solar. K. Fountain. Sci Digest 87:26-9 Ap '80

Great Britain

United Kingdom's approach to energy policy [address, February 4, 1980] N. Lamont. Vital Speeches 46:327-32 Mr 15 '80

921
KOVIC

Kovic, Ron.
    Born on the Fourth of July / Ron Kovic. -- New York : McGraw-Hill, c1976. 208 p. 22 cm.
ISBN 0-07-03539-X

684
HAMMOND

Hammond, James J
    Woodworking technology [by] James J. Hammond [and others. 3d ed.] Bloomington, Ill., McKnight & McKnight Pub. Co. [1972]
    xii, 457 p. illus. 27 cm.

FIC
DIC

Dickson, Gordon R.
    The spirit of Dorsai. Ace Bks [1979]
281 p. illus.

641.5
CADWAL-
LADER

Cadwallader, Sharon.
    Whole Earth cook book [by] Sharon Cadwallader [and] Judi Ohr. Pref. by Paul Lee. Illustrated by Anita Walker Scott. Boston, Houghton Mifflin, 1972.
    xix, 120 p. illus. 23 cm. $3.95 (pbk)

614.58
ENC

The Encyclopedia of mental health.
    Albert Deutsch, ed in chief; Helen Fishman, executive ed. Mini-print Corp 1970 [c1963]
2228 p.

001.6
WEL

Wels, Byron G.
    Personal computers; what they are & how to use them, by Byron Wels. Prentice-Hall [c1978]
193 p. illus. (Trafalgar House bk) (Spectrum bk)

IN-TEXT CITATIONS

There are two basic areas where the works cited will appear, in the text and on the Works Cited page. The Modern Language Association (MLA) has established a standard style for in-text citing of a reference, and it is now in more general use than the footnote system. The MLA's in-text system requires two items in the citation, the author's name and the page number. The idea is to work the reference directly into the text; see below.

1. Signal the beginning and end of quotations or paraphrases. If convenient, begin with the authority's name and end with the page reference.

e.g. Gary North argues that Christians are dead to sin because they can escape its deadly effects since Christ has rescued them (107).

You will note that the authority is given first while the page number appears in parenthesis at the end of the sentence previous to the period. These variations are acceptable.

e.g. Gary North (107) argues, "We are dead to sin because we can now escape its deadly effects."

or Gary North states on page 107 that Christians are dead to sin since they escape its deadly effects.

2. If the authority cannot be introduced with the material, it is acceptable to put both the authority and the page number in a parenthetical citation.

e.g. Paul is saying in Romans 6 that Christians are dead to sin because they are free of its deadly effects (North 107).

3. Keep page numbers outside of quotations but within the final period.

e.g. When North speaks of Christians and sin, he argues, "We are dead to sin because we can now escape its deadly effects" (107).
or "We are dead to sin," argues North (107), "because we can now escape its deadly effects."

4. Introduce sources that have no author listed.

e.g. One regional magazine located the old Jesuit city of St. Gall as the modern city of Fort Stockton ("Crossroads" 49).

or The magazine *Southern Living* located the old Jesuit city of St. Gall as the modern city of Fort Stockton, Texas ("Crossroads" 49).

It is important to see that each time a source is used, it should be given credit.

e.g. One authority points out that sin "is in the whole fabric of our being" (North 107). Another says that sin is the ruination of man (Henry 406).

Other methods exist, particularly the name-year system; it asks for the year of publication. Find out what your teacher requires and follow it. Usually some style sheet is provided.

NOTE CARDS FOR PAPERS

There are two types of cards which you will need for writing these papers:
- a) the bibliography or source cards, and
- b) cards containing notes of facts and information.

BIBLIOGRAPHY OR SOURCE CARDS

It is important to keep a separate, complete, and accurate card record of each source of information you consult. Make out the card as soon as you begin to use the source. Copy the information on the card as it appears on the title page using one of the formats below.

BOOK: author (last name, first name middle name or initial)
               book title (underline it)
               essential data: city, publisher, date of publication

1. If two authors are given, cite the first in the manner above, write the word *and*, then put the second author's name in normal order (first name last name).

2. If you do not use the whole book but only one chapter or certain pages, list those pages under essential data.

3. If no author's name is given, use the editor's name and write it as follows: *Last name, first name, ed.* since the *ed.* signifies an editor.

4. If no author or editor is given, the book title will be the first entry on your card.

ENCYCLOPEDIA ARTICLE: author (if given) (last name, first name)

                       title of article (put in quotes)
                       title of book (underline it)
                       essential data: edition by year, volume, pages

MAGAZINE ARTICLE: author (if given) (last name, first name)

                       title of article (put in quotes)
                       title of magazine (underline it)
                       essential data: volume number, date, pages

5. For a newspaper article or editorial, simply use the same style as the magazine article but substitute the name of the paper for the name of the magazine. The date and pages can still be used, but a volume number is generally not found or necessary. In some newspapers it may be necessary to cite the section.

6. You might find it valuable to put the library call numbers of the book on your bibliography cards if you are taking the information from the card file. It will just save you having to write it somewhere else, and it would be handy if you had to come back to look later.

7. The bibliography cards are used for looking sources up, providing information for citing the work correctly in the paper, and providing the information for the works cited page.

NOTE CARDS FOR NOTES

Below are a series of hints or techniques that have helped many others in the past. Utilize them for greater ease in writing your paper.

1. Use three-by-five index cards or four-by-six cards. They are easy to store and can be readily rearranged as needed.

2. Write on one side of the card only. Use the back only for a personal observation but be sure to mark **OVER** on the front of the card.

3. Write only one item or subject on each card. Never have two items or sources on a single card. It defeats easy rearranging of ideas later.

4. If you are doing a major research project and will be using many cards over a period of time, it is wise to use ink since penciled notes tend to smear with repeated shuffling.

5. List the source on the top right of each card. Use the author's last name and page number. It will serve as the quick reference to the full bibliography card and will give the information necessary for in-text citation. Write the source down before you write the note.

6. If you wish to quote the material directly, use quote marks and copy it accurately.

7. Write a full note; use good sentences since abbreviated materials sometimes do not make sense later on. Full sentences can be more easily worked into your rough draft than incomplete notes.

8. If you have general subheads or points in mind, label the card with whatever subhead applies. Such labels are called *slugs* and are useful for rearranging cards at a later date.

9. Don't take down the obvious, easily remembered, well known, or general statements. Record only that material which is new and you believe will be useful to you when you write the paper.

10. When reading or thinking and you have an idea about the paper, make a note card. On the top right where the source would go, write **MINE** to identify it as your idea. Write down those ideas when they come; if you don't, you will surely forget them later.

11. Notes in your own words can either be paraphrases or summaries. The paraphrase says the same as the original but in different words, yours. It is about the same size as the original in length but is in your style instead of the original author's. The summary is really a précis; that means it is quite reduced in size from the original.

12. The following are items which would need citation of the source:

    a) an original idea derived from a source, quoted or not
    b) factual information from a source, such information not being common knowledge
    c) wording that is exceptional in expression or style, even if it is common knowledge
    d) any exact wording copied from a source
    e) your summary of original ideas from a source

MAJOR PAPER PROCEDURES

GATHERING INFORMATION

1. finding sources:
    A) general - home, school, friends, public library, church, stores (new & used)
    B) specific – reader's guide, indexes, table of contents, encyclopedias

2. skim/hi-grade information: look for what seems to be useable & available
NOTE: your sources are now established.

3. make bibliography card for each source: include author's full name
                                                     title of book/magazine & article title
                                                     page numbers utilized
                                                     publisher
                                                     copyright/publication date
                                                     personal shorthand identification
                                                     any comment about the source (bias, outdated, etc.)

4. make note cards for **each** idea or quote: include   shorthand identification of source
                                                          page number(s)
                                                          quote or idea in own words

NOTE: an easy way to put ideas into your own words is to summarize each paragraph into a single sentence of no more than 15 words. This sentence should reflect what you think is the most important idea in the paragraph.

5. Continue to make note cards until all sources are exhausted. You will have one note card for each separate idea and one note card for each separate quote. You will also have a separate stack of cards for your bibliography; each source will have its own bibliography card. Once you have a bibliography card and the note cards finished for a given source, you will not need to consult that source again.

PUTTING INFORMATION TOGETHER

At this point all sources are gone, and you will use only your cards to write your paper.

1. Separate note cards from bibliography cards.

2. Put all note cards out so that you can see them.

3. Identify basic topic areas, and put all cards which fall under the same topic in the same pile. Label the pile with a piece of paper if you want.

4. After most cards (80%+) are used up, put the leftovers in a separate pile.

5. Arrange the piles, except the leftovers, in the order that you think is best for using them. Often a natural order presents itself; such common orders are based on importance, cause & effect, time & space, or some other logical organization.

6. Treat each pile separately. Go through each pile and find the items which are alike, pick the best card in the mini-group, and label it **common**. Such a label means that it is generally not worth a footnote. The similar cards in the mini-group may be put aside and probably will not be used.

7. Now arrange the cards in the pile into a natural order among themselves. Such an order again may be obvious. If not, suit yourself, but make sure the ideas will flow together. Each pile will represent a paragraph in your paper.

8. The leftovers will be used for extras in the introductory and concluding paragraphs in your paper.

WRITING THE PAPER

1. Write a **THESIS STATEMENT** based on two things:
   A) your purpose - the **why** of your paper, the point you are trying to make and
   B) the **outline** of your paper - the pile topics in the order you will treat them.

2. Write the body paragraphs from the piles you have. Each body paragraph should have a topic sentence; it will usually make reference to the pile topic you are using. Each card should be worth one sentence. Make sure the sentences flow together. Here is where good organization of the pile really helps.

3. Now write an introductory paragraph. It should begin with an interest catcher and work down to the thesis statement. You might be able to work in some of the ideas from your leftover stack. The first sentence is general but catchy. From there on down, the sentences lead to your very specific thesis statement.

4. At this point write the concluding paragraph. The first sentence should be a restatement of the thesis statement or a summary. Again you might be able to use an idea or two from the leftover stack, but be careful not to inject new material, ideas that don't go along with the rest of the paper. Your final statement should be a generalization. Never end on a question unless it asks the reader for a commitment.

5. Let it sit for a few days if possible; then proofread it for error and logic. Correct the errors and rewrite the paper into the finished draft.

6. The finished draft should be double-spaced. Double-spaced lines on your paper make it easier for your teacher to read and comment upon the paper. It will also be easier for you to read the comments. In fact, with the space available between the lines, your teacher will often write a comment directly at the spot with which the comment is associated.

ENDNOTES

Label this page with the word *NOTES* centered and one inch from the top. Continue your page numbering sequence in the upper right corner. Double space between the page heading and the first note. The notes should be numbered in sequence with raised superscript numerals to match those placed in the text at appropriate locations. Double-space all lines both within and between the entries.

Endnotes conform to the rules found below.

1. Two kinds of notes exist: content and reference. A) Content endnotes are generally not used much except in scholarly works. Important information is placed directly in the text; unimportant or marginally related items should be left out entirely. I include the information here simply to give you a working acquaintance with them. B) Reference or documentation endnotes are unnecessary if you do in-text citations. Reference endnotes are favored by some instructors, however, so some examples will be given here for your edification.

2. Endnotes are placed on a separate page(s) from everything else following the last page of the text and prior to your Works Cited page.

3. Place the superscript numerals within the text by turning the roller of the typewriter so that the Arabic numeral strikes about half a space above the line. A computer and printer combination can use the superscript mode. The numeral immediately follows the material to which it refers, usually at the end of a sentence, with no space between the numeral and the end punctuation.

example   ...the tests had similar parameters.[1]

4. Complete documentation to endnotes sources must be found on the Works Cited page. You can mention a work in your endnotes that is not used as an in-text citation, but fully document it on the Works Cited page.

5. Information of the following types appear in content endnotes:

   a) related matters not germane to the text
   b) blanket citation
   c) literature on a related topic
   d) major source requiring frequent in-text citations
   e) comparison of textual commentary with another source
   f) explanation of tools, methods, or testing procedures
   g) provision of statistics (also handled by appendices)
   h) acknowledgment of assistance or support
   i) explanation of variables or conflicts in evidence

6. Reference endnotes generally contain the author's last name, a page number, and sometimes a significant portion of the title of the work if the author has more than one work listed on the Works Cited page.

A note of caution is in order here: some instructors will request footnotes while others will want a superscript number in the text with full documentation in the endnotes along with any comment you might have to make. Whatever your instructor requires is what you should do. Some style sheet is generally given, so be sure to ask for and follow it.

[1] The text also contains a series of charts and tables which graphically display $1000 dollar investments over various periods of time.

[2] On this point see also Beckman (198), Marshall (32-35), Konrad (152), and Wallenstein (64).

[3] On this point see North (3-10), DeMar (214), and Rushdoony (142-144).

[4] All citations of Shakespeare are from G. B. Harrison's edition.

[5] For additional information on this topic, see *Cycles of War* by R. E. McMasters, particularly the appendices covering epistemology, law, and education.

[6] Compare this with Carl Schuster who argues, "The essence of modern investing is to be on top of your portfolio at all times so that you can move in a minute. Long term investing today is archaic with computer trades, on-line services, and immediate access to real time information."

[7] Water samples were drawn from the identical spot each day at 8 a.m., noon, 4 p.m., and 8 p.m. with testing done immediately on site.

[8] This information was reduced to its current form due to the software program developed especially for this application by Vern Julien.

[9] North, p. 107.

[10] *Ibid.*, p. 110.

[11] Tyack, *Managers of Virtue*, p. 223.

Numbers 9-11 are reference endnotes. Full documentation would appear on the Works Cited page. Note number 10 refers to note number 9; note number 11 means that Tyack would have two works referenced on the Works Cited page and that this reference is from the *Managers of Virtue*.

The above is a brief sample of how endnotes according to the style presented here should appear. Styles vary on this, so be sure to check with your instructor to see that you are providing the endnotes in the format which is required. Many books have endnotes that combine content and documentation; it is a popular style. Remember, you are writing for your instructor, so find out what the instructor wants and deliver as best you can.

ABBREVIATIONS

Abbreviations should be used regularly and consistently in notes and citations, but they should be avoided in the actual text of your paper.

In documentation areas always abbreviate the following:

>   dates: Jan., Feb., and so forth
>   states: CA, OR,   use the postal abbreviations

Below you will find some commonly used abbreviations and their meanings. They are for your reference.

AD   *anno Domini,* means "in the year of the Lord" and precedes numerals with no space between the two letters as in "AD 1776"

anon. anonymous

BC   means "before Christ" and follows numerals with no space between the letters as in "500 BC"

ca./c. *circa,* means "about;" used to indicate an approximate date as in "ca. 1850"

cf.   *confer,* means "compare" one source to another; not to be used for "see" or "see also"

ed./eds. editor(s), edition, edited by

e.g.   *exempli gratia,* means "for example," preceded and followed by a comma

esp.   especially, as in "110-115, esp. 103"

et. al. *et alii,* means "and others," "Al Johnson et. al." means Al Johnson and other authors

f./ff.   page or pages following a given page; "8f." means page eight and the following page; "45ff." means page forty-five and pages following; "45+" is also acceptable; exact references might be better: "45-47, 50, 52"

ibid.   *ibidem,* means "in the same place," in the immediately preceding title, used for referencing, normally capitalized and underlined or italicized as in "Ibid., p. 45"

i.e.   *id est,* means "that is," preceded and followed by a comma

illus.   illustrated by, illustrations, or illustrator

loc. cit. *loco citato,* means "in the place (passage) cited"

op. cit. *opere citato,* means "in the work cited," used for a previously cited work

p./pp. page or pages; do not us "ps." for pages, use "pp."

passim "here and there throughout the work" as in "56, 65, et passim" also acceptable is "56+"

sic   "thus" placed in brackets to show an error in the original quoted passage which the writer knows is wrong but is quoting exactly "He and his brother was [sic] going...."

viz.   namely

vol./vols. volume(s), as in "vol. 3"

ANNOTATED WORKS CITED / BIBLIOGRAPHIES

Annotations are simply notes that are affixed to the reference given. These are comments by the writer to give the reader some further information about the source material and reflect the writer's perception of some part of the source material. Below are five types of information commonly found in annotations.

1. The writer might comment on the bias or position of the source material.

2. The writer may make a statement identifying the basic thesis of the source work.

3. Any unique circumstances or credentials regarding the author and the work cited may be identified. This usually is done to either prove or attack the credibility of the author or the source material.

4. At times the writer may identify any major failing or lack in source material, or the writer might comment on the newness or groundbreaking nature of the source.

5. The writer may indicate a possible audience for the work, who would or should be interested in reading the material or using it as a source.

Annotations should not be longer than three sentences. Just provide enough information so that your reader will know the extra item or two that you thought necessary to include. Annotations describe some essential detail. Place annotations just below the normal facts of publication. See the examples below. What you are doing in providing a service to the reader to help them decide if your source is something they might want to rely on or take the trouble to look up and read for themselves.

Bulfinch, Thomas. *Bulfinch's Mythology*. 2 vols. New York: Mentor, 1962. This is a standard work

    that covers Greek, Roman, and Norse mythology.

Costain, Thomas B. *The Chord of Steel*. New York: Doublday, 1960. Costain provides some

    interesting insights into Alexander Graham Bell's life which help to understand both his struggle

    and his victory over the complexities surrounding the invention of the telephone.

APPENDIX / APPENDICES

The appendix is found under particular circumstances and can greatly aid in the understanding of the reader. As the name suggests, it is something appended or added on to the general report.

1. The appendix contains material not directly placed in the text but of value in making or illustrating some point found in the text itself.

2. Material usually found in appendices is not generally text but may be. The forms listed below are common.

   a) charts
   b) graphs
   c) tables
   d) maps
   e) pictures
   f) diagrams
   g) lengthy quotes or entire source documents

3. Material in the appendix should be referred to in the text. The first method given below is preferable.

   a) Direct reference: an actual statement in the text to refer the reader to the appendix

   e.g.   The accompanying graph in Appendix B will further illustrate....

   b) Footnote or endnote reference: in the text a footnote or endnote number is given; the footnote or endnote will refer the reader to the proper appendix. This is a bit cumbersome in that the reader has two directives instead of one.

4. Only one item is normally contained per appendix.

5. The appendices come between the text and the Works Cited (bibliography) page.

6. Appendices have consecutive page numbers with the text.

7. Each new appendix should have its own sheet and a title such as *Appendix A*, *Appendix B*, and so forth. If you only have one appendix, the simple word *Appendix* is sufficient.

8. Each appendix will include two things below the chart, graph, etc.

   a) information necessary to interpret the chart, graph, etc.
   b) the source of the chart, graph, etc.   source documentation should appear on the Works Cited page.

Appendix B

Lump Sum Investment Value Table

	5th yr	10th yr	15th yr	20th yr	25th yr	30th yr	35th yr	40th yr
1%	10,510	11, 046	11,609	12,201	12,824	13,478	14,166	14,888
2%	11,040	12,189	13,458	14,859	16,406	18,113	19,998	22,080
3%	11,592	13,458	15,579	18061	20,937	24,272	28,138	32,620
4%	12,166	14,802	18,009	21,911	26,658	32,433	39,460	48,010
5%	12,762	16,288	20,789	26,532	33,863	43,219	55,160	70,399
7%	14,025	19,671	27,590	38,696	54,274	76,122	106,765	149,744
10%	16,105	25,937	41,772	67,274	108,347	174,494	282,024	492,592
15%	20,113	40,455	81,370	163,665	329,189	662,117	1,331,755	2,678,635
20%	24,883	61,917	154,070	383,375	953,962	2,373,763	5,906,682	14 million
25%	30,517	93,132	284,217	867,361	2,646,698	8,077,935	24 million	75 million

The above table represents the end of the year values for a $10,000 lump sum investment compounded annually at varying investment rates. The percentage at which the investment increases each year is given by the far left hand column beginning with 1% and going to 25%. The years invested are given across the top and are in five year increments. Thus, the table is simple to read; a $10,000 investment that yields 7% per year will be worth $38,696 at the end of 20 years. Source: Van Caspel (17).

The above is an example of an appendix. Note that the source is given last. The author's last name is sufficient since the complete documentation is on the Works Cited page. The number in parentheses is the page number from which the chart came.

SECTION 7

PARAGRAPH PARAMETER CHECK   TYPE 1

_____ name

1. Organization
_____ topic sentence - states purpose/topic of paragraph
_____ subsidiary sentences fit the format
_____ final sentence wraps up, concludes, sums up the paragraph

2. Mechanics
_____ spelling
_____ punctuation
_____ usage

3. Style
_____ sentences flow together well
_____ individual sentences worded well
_____ general impression is positive
_____ balance in presentation
      (sentence length/ideas roughly equal)

4. Content
_____ main idea clearly identified
_____ secondary ideas suitable for subject
_____ good use of material/facts

NOTE: mechanics   0-1 mistake/item/paragraph = +1
                   2-3 mistakes = 0 pts
                   4+ mistakes = -1

GRADE

10-11 = A
8-9 = B
6-7 = C
5   = D

COMMENTS:

PARAGRAPH PARAMETER CHECK   TYPE 2

_____ name

1. Organization
_____ 7 sentences
_____ topic sentence states purpose/topic
_____ body sentences fit the format
_____ good balance (length/ideas)
_____ final sentence wraps up/concludes

+1 0 -1

4-5 = +1
2-3 = 0
0-1 = -1

2. Mechanics
_____ spelling
_____ punctuation
_____ usage

+1 0 -1
0-1 = +1
2-5 = 0
6+ = -1

GRADE

4 = A
3 = B
2 = C
1 = D

3. Content
_____ main idea clearly identified
_____ topic/ideas suitable for format

+1 0
2 = 1
1 = 0

4. Style
_____ reads well, smooth flow, positive impression

+1 0

COMMENTS:

5 PARAGRAPH ESSAY CHECK SHEET

ORGANIZATION

_____ opening statement

_____ general to specific

_____ thesis: purpose clear

_____ thesis: outline/3 topics

_____ topic sentence #1

_____ transition #1

_____ topic sentence #2

_____ transition #2

_____ topic sentence #3

_____ transition #3

_____ restatement of thesis, positive

_____ 2nd sentence summary BP#1

_____ 3rd sentence summary BP#2

_____ 4th sentence summary BP#3

_____ final statement = appeal, etc.

GRADE

A = 5 - 6

B = 4

C = 3

D = 1 - 2

MECHANICAL ERRORS

0 - 2 = +1

3 - 5 = 0

6+ = -1

ORGANIZATION

14-15 = +3

12-13 = +2

10-11 = +1

9 or less = 0

EXPRESSION/CONTENT/READABILITY

2 = very good

1 = average

0 = poor/needs improvement

COMMENT:

ORGANIZATIONAL FORMAT: STUDENT ASSESSMENT FORM

_____ author of paper   _____ evaluator

_____ evaluator   _____ evaluator

PROCEDURE FOR CHECKING ORGANIZATIONAL FORMAT

1. Read the last sentence of the first paragraph to see if it contains both purpose and method; fill in the appropriate blanks below. (purpose line and the second column of this sheet)

2. Read each topic sentence in the body and check the appropriate line if the topic sentence ties directly to the thesis statement. (left column of sheet)

3. Compare the first sentence of the final paragraph with the thesis statement on a point by point basis; check off all repeated ideas. (third column of sheet)

4. Check all internal sentences of the final paragraph to see that they summarize the body paragraphs in the proper sequence; check the proper blanks if they do so. (fourth column of sheet)

5. To check transitions read the closing and opening sentences in each pair of consecutive paragraphs; for each pair write either the transition word or phrase, usually adverbials found in the first sentence of a paragraph, or the connecting idea, usually a noun which is mentioned in both sentences. (blanks at bottom of sheet)

6. Read the introductory paragraph. Decide if the first sentence is a good eye catcher and appropriate for the content of the rest of the paper; rate it 1, 2, or 3 with 3 being very good, 2 being acceptable, and 1 not doing the job. Then decide if a logical progress is made from a general statement in the eye catcher to the specifics of the thesis statement; check the appropriate category.

purpose of paper _____

topic sentences	method/outline	restatement	summary
_____	1._____	_____	_____
_____	2._____	_____	_____
_____	3._____	_____	_____

transitions: introductory paragraph

1/2 _____   1   2   3   eye catcher

2/3 _____   ___ yes ___ no   general to specific

3/4 _____

4/5 _____

BOOK REPORT CHECK SHEET: FICTION

_____ STUDENT NAME

Intro paragraph

____ interest catcher   Set up some sort of grading scale to suit yourself on this one.

____ title

____ author

____ publisher

____ copyright

____ genre (type)

____ # of pages

Thesis statement

____ purpose

____ outline/overview

Body

____ topic sent/bp#1   These 3 body paragraphs would vary depending on the order of

____ setting: time/place   the argument and what three general categories are selected

____ characters   by the student in his/her thesis. These are just suggestions.

____ plot summary   You may want to inject your own guidelines.

____ topic sent/bp#2

____ main point of book

____ author's bias

____ biblical principles

____ justification

____ topic sent/bp#3

____ knowledge gained

____ possible personal use

Final paragraph

____ restatement/summary

____ summary of BP#1

____ summary of BP#2

____ summary of BP#3

____ final statement/recommendation/generalization

MECHANICS: ___ SPELLING   ___ USAGE   ___ MINOR PUNCT.   ___ MAJOR PUNCT.

OVERALL IMPRESSION/COMMENT:

LETTER WRITING CHECK SHEET

_____ name

FORM

_____ heading
_____ date
_____ inside address
_____ salutation
_____ complimentary close
_____ signature
_____ proper spacing
_____ proper alignment flush left

CONTENT

1st body paragraph
_____ friendly opening
_____ states purpose of letter clearly
_____ doesn't give details

2nd body paragraph
_____ gives 1-3 supporting details or statements

3rd body paragraph
_____ restates purpose
_____ includes call to action/indicates response

MECHANICS (number of errors)

_____ spelling
_____ punctuation
_____ usage
_____ any other errors

OVERALL IMPRESSION/COMMENT:

FORM
7 - 8 = +1
5 – 6 = 0
0 – 4 = -1

CONTENT
5 – 6 = +1
3 – 4 = 0
0 – 2 = -1

MECHANICS
0 -1 = +1
2 – 5 = 0
6+   = -1

OVERALL IMPRESSION
good to excellent   = +1
acceptable   = 0
needs lots of work   = -1

GRADE
A = 3-4
B = 2
C = 1
D = 0
F = -1 or below

RESUME CHECK SHEET

_____ name

FORM

heading
_____ at the top
_____ centered
_____ full address
_____ phone number
_____ spaced correctly

objective
_____ first category after heading
_____ active verb

general
_____ categories on left
_____ professional skills
_____ experience
_____ accomplishments
_____ other categories
_____ correct spacing
_____ looks balanced and clean

CONTENT

_____ objective clear & well stated
_____ personal skills
_____ professional skills
_____ experience
_____ accomplishments
_____ other

MECHANICS (number of errors)
_____ spelling
_____ punctuation
_____ other

OVERALL IMPRESSION/COMMENT:

FORM
12 - 14 = +1
10 – 11 = 0
9 or less = -1

CONTENT
5 – 6 = +1
3 – 4 = 0
0 – 2 = -1

MECHANICS
0 errors = +1
1 error = 0
2+ errors = -1

OVERALL IMPRESSION
good to excellent = +1
acceptable = 0
needs work = -1

GRADE

A = 4
B = 3
C = 2
D = 1
F = 0 or below

MAJOR PAPER CHECK SHEET #1

_____ name

Introduction
_____ opening statement
____ thesis

Body
_____ topic sentence @ paragraph
_____ balance
_____ transitions

Conclusion
_____ restatement/summary
_____ final statement/challenge

Form

0 1 2   title page
0 1 2   works cited

EXPRESSION/CONTENT

2 = excellent
1 = average
0 = not so good

MECHANICAL ERRORS

0 - 2 = +1
3 - 5 = 0
6+ = -1

ORGANIZATON

7 = +3
6 = +2
5 = +1
4 = 0

FORM

3 - 4 = 2
1 - 2 = 1
0 = 0

GRADE

A = 7 - 8
B = 5 - 6
C = 3 - 4
D = 1 - 2

COMMENT:

MAJOR PAPER CHECK SHEET #2

_____ name

Introduction
_____ opening statement
_____ thesis

Body
_____ topic sentence @ paragraph
_____ balance
_____ transitions

Conclusion
_____ restatement/summary
_____ final statement/challenge

Form

0 1 2   title page
0 1 2   works cited
0 1 2   endnotes

EXPRESSION/CONTENT

    2 = excellent
    1 = average
    0 = not so good

MECHANICAL ERRORS

0 - 2 = +1
3 - 5 = 0
  6+ = -1

ORGANIZATON

7 = +3
6 = +2
5 = +1
4 = 0

FORM

5 - 6 = 2
2 - 4 = 1
0 - 1 = 0

GRADE

A = 7 - 8
B = 5 - 6
C = 3 - 4
D = 1 - 2

COMMENT:

MAJOR PAPER CHECK SHEET #3

_____ name

Introduction
_____ opening statement
_____ thesis

Body
_____ topic sentence @ paragraph
_____ balance
_____ transitions

Conclusion
_____ restatement/summary
_____ final statement/challenge

Form

0 1 2 title page
0 1 2 works cited
0 1 2 appendix
0 1 2 endnotes

EXPRESSION/CONTENT

2 = excellent
1 = average
0 = not so good

MECHANICAL ERRORS

0 - 2 = +1
3 - 5 = 0
+6 = -1

ORGANIZATON

7 = +3
6 = +2
5 = +1
4 = 0

FORM

7 - 8 = 2
4 - 6 = 1
3 = 0

GRADE

A = 7 - 8
B = 5 - 6
C = 3 - 4
D = 1 - 2

COMMENT:

PARAGRAPH WRITING TEST

_____ name

DIRECTIONS: Answer all questions to the best of your ability. Write the answers in complete sentences, #5 excepted, and use good grammar, spelling, and punctuation.

1. What position in a paragraph should the topic sentence occupy?

2. Give the two functions of a topic sentence.

3. If you had four points to include in a comparison paragraph, briefly explain how you would order them.

4. Briefly explain the rule regarding tense and point of view as applied to paragraph writing.

5. List the seven different methods of organizing a paragraph that we have studied.

6. Arrange the following into the proper order; use the numbers 1-7.

_____ brainstorm   _____ proofread
_____ write conclusion   _____ write topic sentence
_____ write body sentences   _____ organize ideas
_____ decide on topic

7. On a separate sheet of paper or the back of this paper write a seven sentence paragraph using SONGBIRDS as your topic. Identify in the blank the type of organization you will be using.

_____

TEST - ELEMENTS OF 5 PARAGRAPH ESSAY   NAME_____

DIRECTIONS: Answer all the questions in the space provided. Write complete sentences.

1. Explain about transitions.

2. Mention three important facts about a topic sentence in a body paragraph.

3. Explain the structure and purpose of the introductory paragraph.

4. Explain the structure and purpose of the concluding paragraph.

5. For one of the following items, write down a seven sentence skeleton for a five paragraph essay. Identify the type of essay format you are using, and name each of the seven sentences.

a) Old Testament kings   b) strong writing skills and success in school   c) why/how Scripture helps

Pick your topic and use the form on the back of this sheet.

SEVEN SENTENCE QUESTION

My topic is _____

My method of organization is _____

      name of sentence

#1 _____

#2 _____

#3 _____

#4 _____

#5 _____

#6 _____

#7 _____

6. Please make some comment about your writing skills at this point in time.

ANSWER KEYS

Continuity Exercises

What follows are sample answers. Use good judgment.
1. John did something else.
2. He was a nice boy.
3. Their home was a place of love and contentment.
4. The rose was a fine gift.
5. His mother was quite frail these days.
6. She always liked flowers.
7. The little terrier runs hard but never catches them.
8. Those rabbits are thick in the spring.
9. The field is planted in alfalfa.
10. Our house is also next to a forest on the other side.
11. Alfred has a chauffeur's license.
12. He has driven for the church a long time.
13. Then the children waited patiently to be let off.
14. That bus was brand spanking new this year.
15. The church was where Sunday School was held.
16. Mrs. Grace drove another church bus.
17. Other folks drove their cars to church.
18. It was part of his service each week.

Thesis Statements #1

Check to see if common sense is executed in the thesis statements. General parameters are as follows: 1) only one sentence, 2) both purpose and outline occur, 3) the outline contains three items only, 4) the outline follows a logical pattern according to time, space, or argument, and 5) the three items in the outline are grammatically parallel. Below you will find an example or two as well as some comments. The examples are just that; other answers will be equally acceptable.

1. *This paper will review willow, fir, and oak firewoods to decide which is best to burn for fuel.* Note the order; it goes from worst to best fuel wood.
2. Here look for only three items; four are given in the problem, and the student must combine two of them.
3. In this one *lack of dams* should probably be last in the order since the other two reasons could be mitigated or even canceled by dams.
4. Note the order on this one; it should be obvious.
5. *The Honda Prelude and the Ford Taurus will be compared according to appearance, mileage, and price in order to pick the best deal.* Here the two cars should be specific. The order will vary depending on what the student deems important.

Word Economy #1

The following answers are examples of correct responses; they are not the only possible response.

1. Turn right at State Street.
2. He worked carelessly.
3. The Chihuahua is a hairless dog.
4. Bluebeard was a heartless, soulless monster.
5. He approaches his problems childishly.
6. The tiny kitten is a sight.
7. The car snailed up the hill.
8. Speak with emphasis on important ideas and words.
9. Cut unnecessary words from your writing.
10. Dutifully correct wrong statements.
11. They bought an unmanageable horse.
12. The red-hatted girl is my cousin.
13. Your dance conduct was shocking.
14. It was a warm, romantic, moonlit evening.
15. If it could talk, the 92nd Street house might reveal many secrets.
16. We entered the darkened house noiselessly.
17. He opened the door with a welcoming smile.
18. He was always cheerful.
19. The penniless, old man refused my gift.
20. This tool is multiuse.
21. I overnighted in a rat-infested warehouse.
22. The startling news abruptly changed our plans.
23. He likes unsweetened coffee.
24. This test is beautiful.
25. Though he is a recent immigrant, he speaks unaccented English.

Word Economy #2

1. Good company requires the best manners.
2. He spoke repetitiously.
3. Last night was sleepless for me.
4. Consensus is we should rehearse daily for two weeks.
5. The play's premiere broadcast was 16 December at 10 p.m.
6. Evidently we must operate immediately.
7. Unfortunately we arrived in the rainy season.
8. Tony is a talented pianist.
9. He was awarded the medal posthumously.
10. She faced me sadly and spoke drearily.
11. I remember when I liked jazz exclusively.
12. The desire for admiration is universal.
13. He will call when he finishes.
14. Modernizing your home is easy.
15. The storm drove the golfers to shelter.
16. John became a miserly hermit in New Jersey.
17. American women spend millions annually beautifying themselves.
18. For Christmas Aunt Tillie sent me a hand-painted tie.
19. Practice will better your play. (Practice makes perfect.)
20. Some people ate peanuts during the play.
21. Hitler was a merciless man.
22. Your decision is unjust.

ANSWER KEYS

Précis Writing #1

Please note that student answers will vary in expression but what is said should be similar.

1. The first man gathers information impersonally; facts are external. He is a pedantic teacher. The second man integrates concepts and acquires culture. He is a stimulating advisor.

2. Individuals, not the government, are responsible for themselves and their country according to Americanism.

3. Lazy readers are poor readers. Good readers are reflective; they concentrate and work at reading by thinking about it.

Précis Writing #2

1. The liberally educated is physically fit, has a keen intellect for detail and concept, understands his culture, enjoys life without excesses, and loves beauty in all things. He is at one with his universe and can explain it.

2. Developmental reading reduces reading to a technical exercise, denies the full experience to readers, and wastes a teacher's time.

3. Modern Christians do not agree on the relationship of the Law and the Gospel, but understanding that relationship impacts how a believer lives, so a proper understanding is critical.

Sports Rule the Mind

1. Sports cause multiple absences from class.
2. His tally averages 22 hours per week.
3. Janitorial services are disrupted due to sports.
4. Lost school time plus practice time = 42 days per semester.
5. Dollar costs in custodial, secretarial & travel expenses are revealed.
6. He expresses the hope of athletic cuts in favor of academics.
7. He traces the rise of athletics over academics in the last 50 years.
8. Public schools can no longer afford to subsidize sports.
9. He presents four arguments in favor of sports.
10. "No athletics = attendance drop" good, get rid of the losers.
11. "Athletics teaches responsibility & leadership" so do the rest of the subjects without the negatives of sports.
12. "Athletic scholarships" it is better to reward brains.
13. "Community supports sports" only because it's on the cheap, no direct cost.
14. Make sports private enterprise.
15. Lists positives for community if sports are privatized.
16. Let sports thrive or die on their own merit.
17. Teachers will be hired to teach, not coach.
18. Academics & other courses (including PE) will flourish.
19. It is wrong to compare sports & academics in popularity.
20. Academics separated from sports will be able to do its job.

Paragraph Writing Test

NOTE: The answers given are correct but are not written in the form required on this test.

1. the first one
2. a) identify the topic
   b) give the purpose or direction
3. least to strongest
4. once adopted must remain constant
5. example, classification, definition, process, analogy, cause and effect, comparison
6. order top to bottom, left column first 2, 6, 5, 1, 7, 4, 3
7. 1 pt for seven sentences
   3 pts for form, 1@ for topic sentence, body, & conclusion
   1 pt for general content
   mechanics: +1 = 0-2 errors, 0 = 3-6 errors, -1 = 7+ errors
   6 total points possible for this question

TEST GRADING SCALE
A = 11-13
B = 9-10
C = 6-8
D = 3-5
F = 2 or less

ANSWER KEYS

Test - Elements of 5 Paragraph Essay

NOTE: the points per answer will be given along with the essence of the answer only.

1. (3 pts) a) function: bridge the gap, smooth the flow, help
   reader stay with argument
   b) placement: 1st sentence of paragraph or end of
   preceding paragraph & 1st sentence of next
   c) type: connectives - *first, next, finally*
   reference: pronouns, repeats, synonyms that tie
2. (3 pts) a) placement: is 1st sentence of paragraph
   b) function: introduces topic of paragraph
   c) references one of the subjects of the thesis
3. (3 pts) a) structure: general to specific, eye-catcher to thesis
   b) purpose: gets reader's attention
   focuses the point of discussion
4. (4 pts) a) purpose: wraps up the essay
   b) structure: 1st sentence restates thesis
   2nd-4th sentences summarize body paragraphs
   5th sentence makes an appeal or final statement
5. the seven sentence section, page 2 (21 pts)
   1pt for the name of each sentence
   eye-catcher, thesis, topic sentence BP#1, topic
   sentence BP#2, topic sentence BP#3, thesis
   restatement, conclusion/final statement
   2pts for each sentence itself: grade on mechanics &
   appropriate content, transition, etc.
6. (1pt) expression, mechanics, etc.

TEST GRADING SCALE
A = 32-35
B = 28 - 31
C = 23 - 27
D = 18 - 22
F = 17 or less

Works Cited Practice Page

See the next page for this item.

Works Cited

Cadwallader, Sharon, and Judi Ohr. <u>Whole Earth Cook Book</u>. Boston: Houghton Mifflin, 1972.

Commoner, Barry. "Barry Commoner." <u>Rolling Stone</u> 1 May 1980: 44-48.

Cook, E. "Charting Our Energy Future: Progress or Prudence?" <u>Futurist</u> 9 Apr. 1980: 64-69.

Deutsch, Albert, ed. <u>The Encyclopedia of Mental Health</u>. Mini-print Corp, 1963.

Dickson, Gordon R. <u>The Spirit of the Dorsai</u>. Ace Books, 1979.

Fountain, K. "China Updates Ancient Energy--With Emphasis on Solar." <u>Science Digest</u> Apr.
1980: 26-29.

Gall, N. "Elasticity Snaps." <u>Forbes</u> 28 Apr. 1980: 59-60.

Hammond, James J. and others. <u>Woodworking Technology</u>. Bloomington: McKnight &
McKnight, 1972.

Kovic, Ron. <u>Born on the Fourth of July</u>. New York: McGraw-Hill, 1976.

Lamont, N. "United Kingdom's Approach to Energy Policy." <u>Vital Speeches</u> 15 Mar.
1980: 327-332.

"No Shortage of Ideas to Solve the Energy Crisis." <u>U.S. News & World Report</u> 12 May
1980: 70-71.

Wels, Byron G. <u>Personal Computers; What They Are & How to Use Them</u>. Prentice-Hall, 1978.

Williams, R.H. and M.H. Ross. "Drilling for Oil and Gas in our Houses." <u>Technology Review</u>
Mar./Apr. 1980: 24-36.

The above is the key to the exercise on Works Cited. Be careful to note that all items are in the correct alphabetical order. Then check to see that each entry has the correct information in the correct order. Next make sure that the punctuation is correct, the commas, colons, periods, quotes, and so forth. Those titles that are underlined in this example may also be in italics. Either method is correct, but only one method should be used throughout. Finally check the spacing and indentation. Those who use a regular typewriter will use more space due to the nature of the spacing; many of the entries will take up two lines. This exercise is a lesson in attention to detail, but it is important since incomplete information is often insufficient when attempting to locate a source.

SAMPLE SCHEDULE - 5 PARAGRAPH ESSAYS

Below is your schedule for the section covering five paragraph essay elements and styles. We will spend a total of twelve weeks covering this material.

ESSAY PARAMETERS

1. All essays will be typed, use of computers is fine.
2. All other exercises may be typed or handwritten.
3. All essays are due by noon on the dates published below, no exceptions.
4. All essays will be evaluated and returned with the 5 Paragraph Essay Check Sheet.
5. We will conference individually about each essay you write after it has been returned.
6. All essays must be in good form about appropriate subjects to be acceptable.
7. Some essay topics may be assigned, especially if #6 is not met.
8. Some materials or excerpts from same will be read aloud in class; names will not be mentioned unless the example is positive.

Week #1	thesis statement	
Week #2	introductory paragraph	
Week #3	concluding paragraph	
Week #4	body paragraph, transitions, 7 sentence exercises	
Week #5	example essay	due date = Jan 6
Week #6	classification essay	due date = Jan 13
Week #7	definition essay	due date = Jan 20
Week #8	process essay	due date = Jan 27
Week #9	analogy essay	due date = Feb 3
Week #10	cause/effect essay	due date = Feb 10
Week #11	comparison essay	due date = Feb 17
Week #12	final evaluation & conferences	

NOTE: The above was done for a class that met only once per week. It was difficult on the student in the beginning during the thesis statement exercises. The rest went fairly smoothly.

SAMPLE SCHEDULE - MAJOR PAPERS

Mar 17   title page information, works cited information
                assignment: sample title page, works cited page form

Mar 22   correct assignments, discuss note cards: a) works cited, b) for notes
                assignment: two articles to produce both types of cards from

Mar 31   review/correct cards, discuss major paper procedures
                assignment: Christians & debt paper

Apr 14   collect paper on Christians & debt
                discuss endnotes, in-text citations, & abbreviations
                assignment: nuclear power for electricity paper

Apr 28   collect nuclear power paper
                discuss annotated works cited (bibliographies with notes)
                assignment: pro-life movement paper

May 12   collect pro-life paper
                discuss appendices
                assignment: capital punishment paper

May 26   collect capital punishment paper
                short exam

Short Paper Guidelines:

1) typed, double spaced, one side of the paper only
2) about 1000-1200 words each, text is 3 full pages plus part of a 4th page
3) all papers to have a title page and correct numbering
4) all papers to have at least three sources in the works cited page
5) additional requirements are added in a cumulative fashion

due dates	paper topics	added elements
Apr 14	Christians & debt	title page, works cited page
Apr 28	nuclear power	end notes, in-text citations
May 12	pro-life movement	works cited annotated
May 26	capital punishment	appendices

NOTE: Papers are due by noon on the dates specified; **late papers will not be accepted**. Plan ahead!

You will be expected to use whatever sources you can for information; the public and school libraries are available to all comers. Personal libraries and your church library may also address some of these issues. Do not ask me to loan you materials although I may suggest certain sources. Regular encyclopedias are NOT to be used as sources for these papers.

INDEX

INDEX

From Heart to Page
Putting Ideas to Paper with Helps

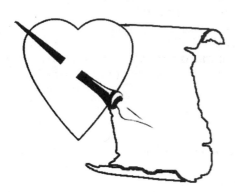

This is a booklet about journaling for young writers. It is designed for grades 4-8 but would be good for any reluctant writer. The book contains topic starters for 180 days. It's great for reluctant writers, young writers, any writer who needs a prompt to get them writing. This easy to use guide helps children move words.

♥ "Michelle Van Loon…makes it easy by suggesting writing prompts for each day. The prompts…are good for all ages and are wide ranging; they deal with events, experiences, observations, feelings, spiritual issues and more. Children who write every day will undoubtedly improve their skills…"
-**Cathy Duffy**, *Christian Home Educators Curriculum Manual*

♥ "It's amazing how many kinds of things there are to write about if you just sit down and think about it. But of course busy homeschooling moms usually don't have that kind of time. I think your booklet provides a real service for people."
-**Jan Burton**, *Editor, Scripture Press*

♥ "It's wonderful! So many ideas…attractively designed, too."
-**Neta Jackson,** *co-author, Trailblazer Books series*

Writing to Change the World
How to Style Your Writing for Publication

Look what you get in this book!

☞ what kind of words to use that grab a reader
☞ how to set up & write various types of articles
☞ tips on plot, character, & details in a short story
☞ what to say in book reviews & who wants them
☞ how to write various kinds of poetry
☞ sample of a query letter and how to write one
☞ exercises to help you practice what you learn
☞ a grade log for you and your teacher

STUDENT: "This book made writing sound so easy. It made me think about becoming a writer. The book made writing sound fun." Ethan Hendricks, 13

HOMESCHOOLING MOM: "As a working and homeschooling mother of five, the self-teach format of *Writing to Change the World* was just what I had been looking for. My eighth and tenth grade sons enjoyed their creative writing lessons more than they ever have before." - Anita Kimball

AUTHOR: "Who knew learning about grammar and punctuation could be so much fun? This guide presents the creative and technical challenges of writing in a series of intriguing, easy-to-follow lessons. I wish I'd had this book when I was first learning to write." Deborah Chester, author of *The King Betrayed*

TEACHER: *"Writing to Change the World* inspires creativity with clear explanations, examples and encouragement. It contains the building blocks to take the students from sentences to short stories confidently and provides both teacher and student with concrete ways to evaluate an abstract subject. It made me want to write something!"
Carol Daugherty, English teacher, 20 years

English Fun Stuff

➤ Pretentious Proverbs - a vocabulary exercise that teaches wise sayings.

➤ Wordhai - a game of extracting three letter words in the right order.

➤ Idioms & Metaphors - over a hundred colorful phrases to decipher.

➤ Flexibility Puzzles - word combinations with a new twist.

➤ Odd and Even - a great game of logic that has infinite replays.

➤ Logic Puzzles - a series of great mindbenders that force careful thought

➤ Single Events - many fun things to do with words, prefixes, and suffixes.

This book is designed to teach, to entertain, and to help the student work with the language or elements of it. My own students enjoyed these games and exercises, and they learned and stretched their minds at the same time. Use the activities in this book as rewards, diversions, complements, fillers, or exercises; you can even grade some of them and give regular or extra credit. The main point is to learn and have fun at the same time.

Sound Spelling

Look what you get in this book!

⊱ an entirely new and effective way to deal with spelling problems
⊱ a lifetime speller, good forever, not just a year or two
⊱ an individualized program that solves your spelling problems
⊱ all the necessary information to become a good speller
⊱ a book based on a reliable, common sense principle
⊱ a series of sound/letter patterns which unlock the keys to spelling

Wordsmiths
1355 Ferry Road,
Grants Pass, OR 97526

Visit http://www.jsgrammar.com for current titles, prices, and other information.

Look at what these folks have to say!

"*Sound Spelling* could easily be called *Spelling for Dummies*. I highly recommend it." Tammy Ryan, editor of *The Homeschool* at www.hschool.com

"I highly recommend *Sound Spelling*, especially for older students who work independently. For younger students, I am confident that the program will be most effective with on-going reinforcement and support from parents." Joan Callaway, Program Director, Be Smart! Tutoring Program, Reading Support Monitor on VegSource Homeschooling Board

"We are happy to recommend it. This was a neat way to learn!" Orilla M. Crider, Director, MATCH, Missouri Association of Teaching Homes

"If you are used to old-fashioned spelling workbooks with lists of words and rules to memorize,...[this] will seem strange at first. But, if you are like so many people for whom the traditional method hasn't worked, setting aside the 'school model' of spelling lessons for a totally new concept that is custom-tailored to your specific needs, will be well worth the effort." D. Keith, Editor of *Homefires: The Journal of Homeschooling* at www.homefires.com

Jensen's Grammar

Your One Stop Source for Learning Grammar

Look what you get in this book!

☞ constant repetition for long term retention
☞ incremental introduction of information
☞ five reproducible reference charts
☞ a comprehensive treatment of parts of speech
☞ the secret of noun & verb cluster syntax
☞ a simple test for prepositions & their phrases
☞ how to make plurals correctly
☞ a quick way to tell linking from active verbs
☞ how to find the main verb in a sentence
☞ two letters that identify almost all adverbs
☞ how to make subjects and verbs agree
☞ all about appositives
☞ a simple list of modals & how they change verbs
☞ derivational & inflectional suffixes explained
☞ instruction in formula writing
☞ the trick that fixes correct usage of *lie & lay*
☞ how to construct passive sentences
☞ secrets of correct compound pronoun usage
☞ a complete & simple summary of verbals
☞ how modifiers can always be identified

Learn how to create, place, and punctuate relative clauses in order to write more sophisticated sentences.

Learn a simple procedure to reduce the number of words in a sentence to help you search for subjects and verbs.

Learn to use a simple chart that unlocks the mystery of differentiating the major parts of speech.

Learn how to actually use the words and structures you are being taught in your own sentences.

Learn the fundamentals of grammar in such a way that you will not forget them but will use them effectively.

Learn the secrets of putting two ideas into one sentence with correct punctuation every time.

Look at what these folks have to say!

"*Jensen's Grammar* is a wonderful program! My daughter went through it and was tremendously helped." Deborah Caskey, homeschooling mom

"I never thought my daughter would grasp subject/predicate breaks or locate nouns, but now she's doing it consistently." Carroll Mantell, homeschooling mom

"When my daughter used it, she went from testing at a 6th grade level to testing at a 12th grade level while in the 8th grade." Doreen Biffart, homeschooling mom

"My children enjoy working with these books; they are clear yet challenging. Our English program has finally come together." Joan Yager, homeschooling mom

"Thank you so much for *Jensen's Grammar*. My kids love it and so do I. They have learned more in these 20 weeks of school than the past 9 years! It has made English enjoyable for us all." Linda Reed, homeschooling mom

"As a former high school English teacher & a present home schooling mom (4 H.S. kids), I enthusiastically endorse your products." Mary Angel, homeschooling mom

What John Saxon did for math, Frode Jensen does for English.

Wordsmiths
1355 Ferry Road
Grants Pass, OR 97526

Visit http://www.jsgrammar.com for current titles, prices, and other information.

Jensen's Punctuation
A Complete Guide to all your Punctuation Needs

Look what you get in this book!

☞ a punctuation rule book with examples
☞ constant repetition for long term retention
☞ a reproducible card of rules for ready reference
☞ a list of key words that reveal certain rules
☞ exercises taken from classical literature
☞ secrets of compound sentence punctuation
☞ how to punctuate long & difficult sentences
☞ when to use commas with subordinators
☞ five simple rules that help immensely
☞ where commas go with a conjunctive adverb
☞ how to use commas with the FANBOYS
☞ when not to use a comma between clauses
☞ how to tell independent from dependent clauses
☞ easy formulas that can be applied continuously
☞ the one word that signals no comma
☞ practice in the use of the comma & semicolon
☞ complete answer keys for exercises & tests
☞ info on grading and scoring exercises & tests

Learn the five basic rules for compound sentences that solve 75-90% of your punctuation problems.

Learn how to use the punctuation index to help you master all the punctuation rules worth knowing.

Learn the three types of key words and how they signal what type of punctuation is needed, if any.

Learn what kinds of words in what kind of situations need capitals and how to identify them in sentences.

Learn when and when not to use a comma with modifiers occurring in various positions in a sentence.

Learn how to correctly use the semi-colon in the most common situation in which it occurs.

Look at what these folks have to say!

"The lessons are quick and painless, about 5-10 minutes each, and you will find these exercises more interesting than what's usually found in grammar texts since they are examples from real books." Teresa Schultz-Jones, national reviewer

"I appreciate the work that went into writing these punctuation books. You have done a good job. I have really seen improvement in my 9th grader's use of punctuation." Joanne Juren, home schooling mom

"I knew there had to be some concrete rules about when and where to apply various punctuation; however, the only instruction I ever got was to just put a comma where you would take a breath. It is a great relief to know the when, where, and why of punctuation, especially when my children want solid answers." Paula Wilcox, home schooling mom

"I am very thankful for the work you have done in preparing these wonderful teaching tools. They are the best I have found." William J. Puderbaugh, Farsight Education

"As a former high school English teacher & a present home schooling mom (4 H.S. kids), I enthusiastically endorse your products." Mary Angel, home schooling mom

What John Saxon did for math, Frode Jensen does for English.

Wordsmiths
1355 Ferry Road
Grants Pass, OR 97526

Visit   for current titles, prices, and other information.

Jensen's Vocabulary

The Easy Way to a Great Vocabulary

Look what you get in this book!

- ☞ constant repetition for long term retention
- ☞ simple format to follow with great results
- ☞ four reproducible charts of roots & affixes
- ☞ a systematic approach to learning vocabulary
- ☞ over 1000 valuable words from basic roots
- ☞ practice based on a proven system
- ☞ daily and weekly reinforcement
- ☞ Latin and Greek based words become easy
- ☞ a complete package for individual or classroom
- ☞ four types of exercises for each set of words
- ☞ easy to follow pattern of instruction
- ☞ little or no teacher input after the beginning
- ☞ easy scoring and test methodologies
- ☞ extensive word parts list for extra help
- ☞ not a free lunch but a great meal
- ☞ better scores on tests like SAT, CAT, etc.
- ☞ easy accountability for teacher and student
- ☞ complete answer keys for exercises & tests
- ☞ increased ability to intelligently guess new words
- ☞ answers to all exercises included for self-scoring

Learn how prefixes, suffixes and roots combine to make all kinds of words.

Learn how to figure out the spelling of a word by the parts that make it up.

Learn how to think in logical fashion about words and their meanings.

Learn a few roots that give you the keys to hundreds of words.

Develop the single most necessary ingredient of good communication: a good vocabulary.

Increase your ability to read and understand as well as express yourself more concisely with these words.

Look what these folks have to say!

"The students increased their vocabulary scores on the Iowa Test of Basic Skills by 22 percent across the board. That means that all students increased their scores. I was elated." Tim Moore, classroom teacher

"I have used your vocabulary books for several years. Not only do my children enjoy the books very much, but they are learning and retaining the information." Karen Locklair, Senior Instructor

"*Jensen's Vocabulary* has proved very useful in expanding my vocabulary. By studying the structure and learning the meanings of the root words, my vocabulary has increased significantly." Christine Dawson, 14, homeschooled student

"After using Jensen's Grammar and Vocabulary: Latin I with our 7th grader, his achievement test scores increased 18% in total language and 45% in spelling from his previous scores. Thank you. We love your books." Derlyze Breitner, homeschooling mom

"As a former high school English teacher & a present home schooling mom (4 H.S. kids), I enthusiastically endorse your products." Mary Angel, homeschooling mom

What John Saxon did for math, Frode Jensen does for English.

Wordsmiths
1355 Ferry Road
Grants Pass, OR 97526

Visit http://www.jsgrammar.com for current titles, prices, and other information.

A Journey Through Grammar Land

A Systematic, Easy to Learn, Tour of Grammar

A modern *Pilgrim's Progress* type allegory that teaches language skills in an enjoyable fashion.

Join Tank and PG as they travel through Grammar Land. Learn with Tank as he meets and interacts with all sorts of people who instruct him and guide him on his journey.

These books cover the Namers and their Substituters. Students will recognize them as Nouns and Pronouns. Then Tank meets with the Tellers or Verbs. Students will easily pick up on proper syntax of helping verbs in combination and also learn who the Linkers are as well as all about the BE family. Later Tank finds out about Adjectives and Adverbs with a trip through the Descriptive Mountains on to the Central Intelligence Adverbial Agency. Learn how Tank and his friends outmaneuver King Falsifier and the renegades in this book. From there Tank learns about Prepositions and Conjunctions. Tour Prepositional Railway Station with him and then go on to Connecting Junction. Tank then moves on to meet the various types of clauses. You will go with him to visit Thought Trucking Terminal where you will learn about simple sentence patterns and from there move on to Clause Village, home of the complex sentence builders. Finally Tank will go to Verbal International Airport where the participles, gerunds, and infinitives are.

CHECK THIS LIST OF BENEFITS FOR YOU & YOUR STUDENT!

✓ Totally self-contained: story, lessons, tests, answers, & teacher helps.
✓ Constant review for long term learning using spaced repetition.
✓ Full story text in front, a grammar synopsis in the back with exercises.
✓ Innovative structure and design, easy to follow presentation.
✓ Minimal teacher preparation time needed.
✓ Successfully used for both initial teaching and remediation.
✓ 5th-7th grades targeted but appropriate for a wide variety of ages.
✓ Solid teaching and coverage of standard material.
✓ An easy yet enjoyable story that teaches about grammar.

> "The Grammar Land books should be useful for a broad range of home schooling situations since they are so user-friendly."   *Cathy Duffy*

Notes from the Smithy...

FREE quarterly electronic newsletter, that's right, yours FREE for the asking.

TWO EASY WAYS TO SIGN UP:

Visit our web site at http://www.jsgrammar.com and follow the prompts.
Email me at frodej@jsgrammar.com and ask to subscribe.

Each issue of "Smithy Notes" contains all original articles on teaching, both practical methods and philosophical overviews. There's news about what's going on with the books and the company, and there's always something fun to do, an exercise or puzzle that you can share with your students.

Wordsmiths
1355 Ferry Road
Grants Pass, OR 97526

Visit http://www.jsgrammar.com for current titles, prices, and other information.